The Rock Warrior's Way

The Rock Warrior's Way

MENTAL TRAINING FOR CLIMBERS

ARNO ILGNER

Desiderata Institute
La Vergne, Tennessee

The Rock Warrior's Way

Published by
Desiderata Institute
315 Oakwood Cove
La Vergne, TN 37086
USA
www.warriorsway.com

Project editor: Jeff Achey

Book design: Painted Wall, www.paintedwall.com

Warrior's Way logo design: Jeff Stamper, www.jeffstamper.com

Library of Congress Cataloging-in-Publication Data

Ilgner, Arno, 1954 -
The rock warrior's way: mental training for climbers / Arno Ilgner
             p.   cm.
    ISBN 0-9740112-0-7
    1. Rock climbing   2. Training—mental   I. Title

Printed in the United States of America by
Vaughan Printing, Nashville, TN
www.vaughanprinting.com

Cover photograph: Arno Ilgner. Insets: Jeff Achey, Jonathan Hollada
Author photograph, page 145: Jeff Achey

Photographers:
Shullphoto, Harrison Shull Photography, www.shullphoto.com
Jeff Achey, www.paintedwall.com
Beth Wald, waldfoto@aol.com
Jonathan Hollada, www.jonathanhollada.com

I dedicate this book to you, a seeker who wants to improve the quality of his climbing experience. Be open, be curious, be observant, and pay attention.

Critical Acclaim for *The Rock Warrior's Way*

"When I was at the peak of my climbing career I didn't fully understand why I was successful. I wasn't stronger physically than other climbers but I knew a passion drove me. Now I know what some of the elements of my success were that I couldn't articulate. Warrior's Way has given me some ideas on how to improve my climbing and my life today. I've read the book twice now and it will be a frequent resource for the future."

—Henry Barber

"This is the first book I've seen that addresses, in depth, the inner game of climbing, and it's about time. In a growing climbing community of specialization, this book gives a new look at climbing and healthy self analysis for almost everyone involved in the sport."

—Jim Bridwell

"As a devoted rock climber, I am always looking for tools to make me more successful. But rarely do I come across a tool as powerful as *The Rock Warrior's Way*. The principles in Arno's book drastically raised my awareness and helped solidify a goal I've been working on for three years—*Flex Luthor*."

—Tommy Caldwell

"Reading *The Rock Warrior's Way* reminds me of my past. This book is full of the tools that I learned to trust during my competition career. I believe this book will help climbers raise their level of power without any additional training."

—Robyn Erbesfield-Raboutou, four-time World Cup sport-climbing champion

"*The Rock Warrior's Way* is an excellent treatise on recognizing and overcoming psychological barriers to reaching one's full climbing potential. Borrowing from a variety of sources, Ilgner has designed a program he calls 'the Seven Processes,' having as its underlying premise the impeccable use of attention. Carlos Castaneda's books about the Indian sorcerer don Juan Matus have long attracted the attention and praise of climbers, and the author has seamlessly woven into his program many of the salient principles taught by this mystical character. Perceiving a climb as a journey, set in motion by intent, is a powerful stimulus for success, as this reviewer can personally attest."

—John Gill

"Warrior's Way identifies and names weaknesses within our intuitive selves. Once a problem is recognized, it becomes a solvable challenge. All climbers will recognize patterns from their own lives within the text."

—Lisa Gnade

"When I first climbed with Arno some 20 years ago, I admired his poise on the rock, his boldness on the lead, and his calm in the face of all obstacles. After reading *The Rock Warrior's Way*, I understand the depth of thinking behind his composure, the inner quiet that frees his mind for pure climbing. He seems to have mastered all the mental demons that hold one back on rock and ice, and this book tells me how to slay them in myself. Now I have a plan: to reread this book and let it transform my climbing from within. Then I'll give it to my partners."

—*John Harlin III, Editor,* American Alpine Journal

"Climbing performance evolves from the inside out and Arno Ilgner beautifully dissects this nebulous subject in *The Rock Warrior's Way*. Drawing on his 30 years of climbing experience as well as a wealth of timeless wisdom, Ilgner presents a compelling seven-step process to becoming a master of your internal mental environment. Consistent, disciplined application of this book's many strategies will not only enhance the quality of your climbing, but it will make you a more skilled risk taker in all aspects of your life."

—*Eric J. Hörst, personal trainer, author of* Training for Climbing

"I have long held confidence in the theories this book describes."

—*Leo Houlding*

"*The Rock Warrior's Way* is a timely contribution to raise our awareness. Arno makes a bold move with a humble approach that reaches for a higher level of life on the rock."

—*Ron Kauk*

"If you can master even a few of the many concepts that Arno Ilgner promotes in *The Rock Warrior's Way*, your climbing may be transformed. The most memorable point to me was Arno's lesson about improving your climbing by learning to deal with falling. This reminded me of Jorge Visser learning the same lesson at the Virgin River Gorge. The last 30-foot section of *Captain Fantastic* (5.13c) is a run-out to the anchors with a subtle but kind of scary finish. (We call that 'salsa.') It is a dramatic, final place to fail with the 13c already well below. Jorge logged a number of 30- to 60-foot falls on this section. His fear of falling turned into a relaxation about falling. He learned to deal with falling and that helped pave an important part of his road to 5.14. He was transformed."

—*Randy Leavitt*

"When the climb is done, what's left? The experience! *The Rock Warrior's Way* will help you choreograph your experience through a full-frontal dance with the beautiful and demanding realities of our sport. You'll learn to relinquish the Ego-driven yearning for external success and recognition, in favor of allowing your spirit its love-driven embrace of climbing and life. This is a landmark work!"

—*Jeff Lowe*

"*The Rock Warrior's Way* describes the amazing potential of human will once the ego is tamed, and is full of insight on honing the mental aspects of concentrated effort. It will help you better understand the spiritual awareness that comes when engaging in a challenging pursuit, and make you more likely to retain that understanding after the adrenaline wears off. This is a great book for learning about the rock climber within."

—*John Middendorf*

"Arno has managed to put into simple words the psychological processes that we struggle with as climbers. Most of us have practiced to various degrees the lessons and principles held within these pages, but none has ever truly mastered them. Arno breaks down the positive and negative chatter that runs through our minds before, during, and after a climb. Then, using climbing analogies we can all relate to, he shows us how to follow our personal paths to greater knowledge, growth, and ultimately success."

—*Scott Milton*

"The mental aspects of climbing can be extremely difficult to master. If used correctly, the Warrior's Way can be more useful than any amount of physical training and can push you to new levels."

—*Beth Rodden*

"In an era where an unhealthy emphasis is placed on tools like rock gyms and campus boards, which train the body, it's refreshing to read a book that addresses the critical but often-overlooked mental component to climbing. Blending firsthand experience from his long, storied climbing career with simple, direct prose, Ilgner offers a serene, process-based way of improving your climbing that avoids the all-too-common pitfalls of anger, stagnation, and frustration. Long a victim of my own reward-based, "redpoint" way of thinking, I now intend to get out, get after it, and celebrate my love for the sport the Rock Warrior's way."

—*Matt Samet, Associate Editor,* Climbing Magazine

"In *The Rock Warrior's Way* Arno Ilgner illuminates the illusive mental states and processes that can hinder or free us to fully experience the purity of climbing. Ilgner touches in on the heart of the matter—who we are inside—and uses this as the foundation for understanding how we relate to the rock. *The Rock Warrior's Way* is an invaluable guide for anyone sincerely looking to have a breakthrough in their approach to climbing."

—*Chris Sharma*

"Finally! A strength-training book for climbers that focuses on the most important power source—the mind.

—*Todd Skinner*

"I thought I had a lot of this stuff figured out, but there were many new ideas in *The Rock Warrior's Way* that I took to heart. The very next day after reading the book I pulled down a boulder problem that had been frustrating me for some time. The power of positive visualization is truly amazing. I would imagine that almost anyone, be they a climber or not, could benefit from reading *The Rock Warrior's Way*."

—*Mark Synnott*

"When you climb big mountains, you will suffer. In alpine climbing the range of my discomfort has included being cold, wet, and fatigued. The pinnacle of the challenge for me, both physically and mentally, has included surviving a severe accident. I learned to accept and embrace it. *The Rock Warrior's Way* helps you understand the need to accept the situation as it is and guide you on how to deal with it."

—*Jack Tackle*

"Arno can teach you to climb consistently at your highest level, no matter the medium. His concepts will keep your mind from straying and your body moving toward your goals. I consciously return to the lessons I learned in his Warrior's Way program while soloing big peaks and clipping bolts."

—*Chris Warner, first American to solo an 8000-meter peak (Shishapangma, South Face)*

"*The Rock Warrior's Way* is a very insightful look beyond the physical side of climbing and into the heart and soul of it—the mind. Climbers of all levels will be able to benefit from Arno's work. I know I have already."

—*Mark Wilford*

"Many of us are blind to our motivations and why we do not perform up to our desires. Reading and embracing the Warrior's Way will certainly change that. The book delves deeply into the inner reaches of our psyche in ways that no other climbing literature has. The Warrior's Way is not simply a guide to improve your climbing, but shows you how to better approach life as a whole."

—*Tony Yaniro*

Acknowledgements

A creative work is never done alone. Our Ego will want to take full credit for it but invariably we've been helped by friends and family, inspired by our heroes, and motivated by challenging experiences. I've had my share of challenging experiences, which forced me to look at the limiting ways I interacted with the world. Working through these experiences was critical in developing this material. My climbing heroes inspired me to push myself on routes, thus giving me the laboratory to test the material presented in this book. For my friends and family I am most grateful.

Jeff Achey has been invaluable in the creation of this work. He was interested in the material in its early stages, in 1996, and introduced it with his articles in *Climbing* magazine. More significantly, he wrote this book, using my notes, stories, scripts, and with much discussion with me before, during, and after the various drafts. His beautiful writing style has created a book that far exceeded my vision of it.

In 1998 I was still in the beginning stages of developing this material. I want to thank all my students during that time, and the climbing gyms where I taught, Atlanta Rocks, Classic Rock Gym, and Climbmax, for their trust and faith in me. Although I feel I added value for the students, my material was a far cry from what it is today.

As I continued to teach and refine the material several people helped me make breakthroughs. Steve Jones helped me identify the core themes in each warrior process and develop effective ways of teaching them. Clay Rubano helped me in many ways, but was specifically important in integrating the graphics of the Bullet and the Laser Beam. Chris Warner helped me see the warrior processes from the inside out, which helped me to be more effective in teaching them. Doyle Parsons has helped me to brainstorm the material throughout the years. He has been a gracious friend, with whom to share ideas and to help me ground my idealistic-type thinking.

I want to thank Rita Bills, Thomas Schmidt, Steve Anderson, and Joe Finnegan for their efforts to edit and proofread the manuscript. I also received valuable suggestions from Steve Petro, Lisa Gnade, Lynn Hill, Ed Webster, Eric Hörst, John Gill, Todd Skinner, Paul Piana, John Long, Jim Gilchrist, Kirk Brode, Lance Brock, Stuart and Heidi Chapin, Jeff Jenkins, Suzy Wilkinson, and my brother Mark.

I appreciate the help of Fred Knapp with Sharp End Publishing and Mike Jones with Wilderness Press for their feedback on the content and layout questions I had. I'd like to thanks Michelle (Kadar) Moore, my first student, whose inquiry helped start me on the path.

Lastly, I'd like to thank Jane, my wife, for her patience during these many years. I sincerely appreciate her belief in me and her support of my desire to create a life's work in my passion.

Thanks again to all.

—*Arno Ilgner, La Vergne, Tennessee, Spring 2003*

Statement of Risk

Important Note to Readers

WARNING: Climbing is inherently risky and can result in injury or death. It's your responsibility to consciously choose what you are willing to do, and to do it from your own motivation. This program is not intended to encourage you to take unacceptable risk, but to give you tools to help analyze and understand risks. Only you can determine what risk is appropriate for you. If you do decide to climb and take risks, I suggest taking small ones. Your goal should be to learn about yourself, not to learn recklessness. Make conscious choices that make sense to you. Don't blindly follow my suggestions or anyone else's.

CONTENTS

Foreword
By John Long

Consider the climber who wants to raise his standard, climb *Astroman* in Yosemite or a route of the next grade at the local crag. Common sense says the direct path to these goals is to practice longer and harder. It's that simple, no?

No.

Everything from ancient wisdom schools to the newer "mental fitness" disciplines insist that transformation is largely a matter of practicing smarter, not simply harder. Practicing harder often results in the reinforcement of limiting habits, meaning, you're just practicing the same old mistakes and reaping the same old results.

Any worthwhile self-improvement program—the Rock Warrior's Way included—allows us to learn from our direct experience in an accelerated way. It will provide a flexible road map to success, which keeps us on course toward mastery and empowers us to make critical course corrections before we find ourselves totally lost in old habits. Such is the essence of practicing smarter. It involves consciously studying the what, the how, and the why of our actual experience. It takes us out of a pure doing mode and requires learning and practicing things that can make us wonder if we haven't taken an awfully indirect route to the mountaintop. As the saying goes, the direct path to mastery is seemingly indirect.

For instance, it might seem questionable that redefining our notion of success could radically steepen our learning curve—but it can. So can other basic tenets of the Rock Warrior's Way. While I won't try to explain the course's content, there are several points worth mentioning that might help orient a person toward sound results.

First, accept that life is hard, and that transforming our life—or our abilities, which amount to much the same thing—is very hard. For a thousand reasons, we all have a part that wants to believe the world was made just for us, and that the pearls of existence are our birthright. In a sense, they are, but we must dive deeply to find those pearls—down past our resistance and mechanical thinking and behavior, and that always involves hard, sustained, conscious, and disciplined effort. Few stumble across those pearls by fluke or good fortune, and if they do, they typically lose them just as fast. This course will head you in the right direction and even give you a stout push that way, but you must do the work.

A colossal swindle of the "New Age" movement is the notion that gaining a state of effortless being and doing requires no effort. In fact, great conscious effort, discipline, and patience are normally required to enter the "flow zone" where previously frightening challenges start taking on an aspect of relaxed ease. The venue does not change. Everest does not get smaller and the North Pole does not get warmer. It is we who must transform, and that takes work. If the process was easy, we'd all be world champions.

Second, the work is a process, and that process lasts a lifetime. Every time you gain a new plateau, a massif of unrealized potential soars above you. In this sense, you never "arrive," once and for all, on the mountaintop. At certain points along the way, the quality of the process changes dramatically. This is especially true for those breakthrough moments of peak performance, where months of sustained effort conspire to create a sort of wormhole of grace through which we pass—often suddenly and with little "effort"—into a higher realm of being and doing. The climb that once spanked us now seems "easy." In such moments we tend to forget the arduous run-up to the crown. It is then that we might recall all of those championship coaches who remind us that the game is won or lost on the practice field.

That leads us to the third and most important point: the qualities you bring to game day will be the exact same qualities you cultivate during practice. In other words, the way you live your life is exactly the way you will climb. It's a simple enough concept to grasp, but taking it to heart and putting it into practice is typically something only the most dedicated can manage; probably because they're the ones whose lives might depend on doing so.

At the recreational level, climbing is often held in an entirely different light than one's "normal" life. The casual climber sees her climbing as a welcome if not essential restorative practice. Half way up the climb, she transcends her daily stressors and morphs into a "different" person. But when she confronts the summit headwall, and her abilities are stretched to the breaking point, the "different" person reverts to old habits. She will meet the challenges with exactly those qualities she's cultivated—usually unconsciously—at work and at home.

When we start pushing the envelope, our most entrenched habits almost always take over. How could it be otherwise? When the river runs smooth, we're all heroes. Only when the big water starts to roar can we find out where we stand and what we're made of. And the key word here is "made." What have we made ourselves?

The Rock Warrior's Way provides a comprehensive program for you to make yourself a more accomplished climber, but only you can supply the means. This requires a conscious effort and an ironclad commitment if those pearls are ever to be fully claimed as your own. One of the shockers of doing any deep work is discovering how little we act and how much we react. And our reactions are steeped in our old fear-driven patterns, with all our survival instincts attached. Breaking loose from these patterns has been likened to freeing yourself from a lion's jaws, and you've little chance of accomplishing this without a strong commitment. We waver, slip, and revert to our comfortable old mechanics. When we realize we've still made some ground despite all the backsliding, we understand that what got us there was our commitment.

This takes us back to the idea that the seemingly indirect path is in fact the direct path to excellence. Here, the "indirect" path requires that you make the Warrior principles your own, that you live them moment to moment, that you practice and hone them in your daily life as well as on the river or on the cliff side.

Put simply, the more you integrate the principles into your daily life, the more powerfully they will work for you on the face of the tidal wave. I've touched on the basic yet often overlooked fact that when we're standing in tall cotton, so to speak, we don't need advanced tools. But when life and limb are at stake, we can never be over prepared. If we prepare by practicing these principles when little is at stake, the lessons become instinctual and will be second nature when the crux is encountered. The boon of all this is that the Warrior principles have been gleaned from enlightened sources and are universal principles for transformation and self-mastery. If I'm going to practice something day in and day out, it's reassuring for me to know that the material is gold by any measure.

This course is not just another of the cut-and-paste jobs we so frequently see in today's endless search for the quick fix or for sudden enlightenment. Arno Ilgner spent years troweling through the world's classic wisdom traditions, as well as many modern modalities, ranging from chaos and systems theory to Voice Dialogue. Through a long process of self-study and trial and error, he arrived at a step-by-step method that allows an adventure athlete to experientially grasp the concepts and to continue the process on his own.

Students of the Rock Warrior's Way should appreciate that, while many of these principles have been around for upwards of 3500 years, the disciples of old never tested them 2500 feet up El Capitan. I can only feel that, seeing today's adventurers taking the qualities of bodymind onto the great rocks of the world, the masters of old must be smiling down from the clouds, knowing their sacred tradition is being carried out in exciting and remarkable new ways.

Finally, any sincere adventurer has, through direct participation, learned to manage fulsome levels of intensity and to maintain a focused mind. Anything beyond advanced-intermediate level climbing requires as much. These capacities put you in good stead to grasp and quickly integrate the course principles and to start enjoying results. While the world might not have been made just for you, the Rock Warrior's Way certainly was.

—John Long, Venice, California, 2002

Preface

Let me reconstruct a climbing experience I had years ago.

"I'll lead this. I can do it! I'll show you how it's done." I climb up some thin moves using underclings and side pulls for handholds, place a solid medium-sized chock, and scan the sequence above. The holds seem indistinct and not straightforward on the vertical wall above. The pro above looks like it will be intermittent and small. I am talking to myself:

"I wish the holds were more obvious. I want to get another pro piece but I don't see where one will fit. I have to do this—I can't go down."

I climb up a bit and see pro possibilities about ten feet higher. My self-talk continues: "I don't know if I can make it. A fall from up there would be dangerous. But I have do it. What will Brian think of me if I just give up? I should at least look like I'm struggling and giving it my all before I fall."

I climb up, not willing to commit myself to going all the way to where the next pro possibilities are, even though the next few moves seem easier. I hesitate.

"Should I commit? I'm getting higher—don't want to fall too far. I'm getting pumped now and feel off balance." To feel more secure, I hold on tighter. "I have to get in some pro here."

I see a wide slot and pull off a hex from my rack, but I can't work it in. "God, why didn't I let Brian lead this? I led the last route. I just want to get a solid piece."

My forearms are flamed, legs shaking. I'm holding my breath. I want to be off this route. "Watch me!" I yell to Brian. I hold on for a few more seconds unwilling to let go of control. Inevitably, too pumped to keep fighting, I give in and take a short fall. The chock I'd placed below holds, arresting my fall and keeping me off the ground.

"What the hell is wrong with me? I suck! I've done plenty of 10s. Who cares about this dumb route, anyway?"

The route was *Super Slab*, a 5.10d in Eldorado Springs Canyon, Colorado. The year was 1977. The book *Climb!* (a history of Colorado climbing) had just come out, which was full of stories of my heroes and the staunch ethic that guided their climbing—no falls, ground up, and no hanging on pro. As I rested, I noticed some friends scrambling up in our direction. "Brian," I called down quietly, "don't tell them that I fell."

This was not one of my finer moments, but I realize now that it was not so unusual. Perhaps you can see in this story ways I was thinking and climbing that limited my performance. Over the years to come—almost twenty-five years, in fact—my way of climbing evolved. I learned to use attention more effectively and climb more decisively. In the past few years, I have fashioned a powerful way of climbing, which I use myself and also teach. I call it the Rock Warrior's Way.

I started climbing in 1973. Aluminum wedges and hexes were just being introduced. Pitons were being phased out as free-climbing protection. Such "clean" climbing was new, and I can still remember free climbing with a sling of chocks, pins and a hammer. Few climbers used chalk and belaying was done mostly via a "hip-belay." I was climbing the limestone and sandstone cliffs of Tennessee while studying geology at Tennessee Tech University.

In 1976 I attended the Army Ranger School at Fort Benning, Georgia, and then transferred to the University of Colorado in Boulder. While in Boulder, I was influenced by my heroes—Roger Briggs, Duncan Ferguson, Jim Erickson, Pat Ament, Steve Wunsch, David Breashears, Henry Barber, and Jim Collins to name a few. I didn't know them personally, but I identified with their approach to free climbing and did my best to emulate their staunch ethic. I worked my way through the grades until I was climbing 5.10s regularly. Being willing to take falls was part of my approach to climbing. There were no sport routes in the 1970s; it was all just climbing. There were plenty of natural lines of weakness—cracks, series of flakes, and thin cracks on faces—that protected with traditional chocks and later cams.

Climbing trad routes, that sometimes can be runout, pushing beyond what you perceive is your limit, assessing fall consequences, taking falls, responding to falls—all these facets of climbing involved engaging risk situations. By engaging risk, I was forced to deal with fear. By dealing with the fear I clarified what the true consequences were and eliminated or reduced illusory fears.

In 1978 I received a BA in Geology from the University of Colorado, but geology was never my passion. What I really loved was climbing. After a tour of duty in the Army, I moved to Wyoming to work in the oil fields. In 1982 the price of oil dropped precipitously and I, along with the majority of oil-field workers, lost my job. I was lost. What do I do now? It seemed that everything had been laid out for me up to this point. After high school I went to college, then I went in the Army to fulfill my obligation, and then I worked as a geologist in the oil field because that's what I studied in college. But what now?

I was forced to look at what I was doing and look at myself. Soon thereafter I moved back to Tennessee to work odd jobs and finally take a position at my father's industrial-tool business. One feeling kept nagging at me: I needed to align my work with my passion.

Working in the tool business was frustrating. I was in a state of divine discontent. I was hitting bottom. The situation was so stressful that changing my beliefs and perceptions suddenly didn't seem so scary. I knew I needed to do something different, so I started looking for help. On the commute to work I began listening to informational and inspirational audiotapes. At home I read numerous philosophy and self-help books. Some of the authors were, George Gurdjieff, Carlos Castaneda, Charles Tart, Robert Spencer, Dan Millman, Chögyam Trungpa, Miyamoto Musashi, M. Scott Peck, Wayne Dyer, Michael Murphy, George Leonard, Jerry Lynch, Gary Zukav, Rick Fields, Anthony Robbins, and Deepak Chopra. For a more complete list of authors, please see the reading list at the end of this book. What I found in my search for meaning was this:

It's our responsibility to create our life's work in something we are passionate about because that is the most effective way we can create happiness in our life. A life's work in "that something" is the best path to challenge us and it's the most effective way to serve others.

I was working in a job that wasn't aligned with what I loved to do, which was climbing. Perhaps I had a negative impression about climbing careers. I felt I was too old to be a top climber. I didn't want to own a climbing store or gym. I didn't want to be a guide all the time, nor did I want to be a manufacturer's representative. I didn't want to do these things, but that didn't change the reality of what I had discovered, which is to create my life's work out of my passion.

So I looked deeper. I looked at my specific talents in climbing. What did I excel in? I decided that my greatest strength was my ability to deal with fear.

By 1995 I had mountains of notes, books highlighted, and stacks of favorite audiotapes. Could I synthesize all this information and create a course to teach fellow climbers? Would anyone be interested in what I had to say? These questions permeated my consciousness. Going through all my material, I looked for core themes. I found them. Key processes kept recurring in slightly different forms. If a person went through one of these processes effectively, he was empowered. If ineffective, he experienced self-limiting thinking and fear. I also recognized that the mass of people do indeed think in a self-limiting way. It made sense that climbers wouldn't be exempt from such behavior.

I identified seven distinct processes. From these discoveries, I began to create my course. I set the goal: to find a way to teach my insight to climbers.

I had exposed myself to many different authors, all of whom had their own particular way of understanding truth and the world. They had their methods and beliefs for the best way to interact with the world and what was most effective. There was the religious approach, the philosophical approach, the scientific approach, the psychological approach, and others. What approach would I use? After reading and listening to overwhelming amounts of information I felt I was drowning in it. I needed some guide for my material.

I read Dan Millman's book *Way of the Peaceful Warrior* and saw strong similarities to the books of Carlos Castaneda. I wrote Dan to ask him where he came up with his approach for his books. I didn't really expect him to answer my letter but one day I received a phone call from him. "Sometimes it's easier for me to just make a call rather than respond by mail," he said. "Did you follow the teachings of don Juan, as Carlos did?" I asked. His answer surprised me; at least it was somewhat unexpected.

"The truth is out there," Dan began. "Look for the truth that underlies everything. Everyone just has a little different way of expressing it. Listen and pay attention."

I paid attention and received an insight early one morning as I was waking up. It would be a powerful clue—one that not only directed me how to proceed, but also showed me the mechanism. As I was waking, in that sometimes-lucid state of half-sleep, I had a persistent thought. I don't know if my higher self was speaking to me or if it was divine intervention, but there it was. "Follow the warrior's way that don Juan talks about in the Carlos Castaneda books." It was just the framework I needed to guide me.

Studying Castaneda's books and other books on warriorship in more depth, I came up with the guiding principle I was looking for. The warrior's way is all about impeccable use of attention. Everything hinges upon how one uses attention—does one waste it or focus it onto the task at hand? This principle was a very pragmatic and tangible guide.

I hadn't reasoned my way directly to this insight. I had gathered information, but the answer itself had come from my intuition. This event further convinced me of something I had been coming to for a while. Solutions involve a unified process, combining conscious analysis, receptivity to intuition, and the discipline to follow through. I refined the Rock Warrior's Way philosophy and method using this insight from that waking moment. By being observant and paying attention, I structured my ideas around a warriorship framework.

So when you reflect on my story of *Super Slab*, do you see anything of your climbing in it? I've now worked with hundreds of climbers, and know those struggles I had in Eldorado are typical and widely shared.

Here are a few questions that will give you insight into what might be limiting your climbing performance:

When climbing a route that challenges you at your limit, do you …

1. … get frustrated when things don't turn out as you want or expect?
2. … hold your breath when you climb?
3. … believe that falling isn't part of the climbing process?
4. … dwell on what's impossible and what you can't do?

5. ... commit only tentatively when climbing into the crux?

6. ... resist falling, over-protect, overgrip, or grab quickdraws/pro?

7. ... rush yourself, think about wanting to be through the crux or at the top of the route, wanting the effort to be over?

Answering "yes" to any of these questions indicates that you aren't using attention impeccably, as a warrior would.

Now, read this book. If you dedicate yourself to the mental effort of adopting the warrior processes, your awareness will improve dramatically. No matter how imperfectly you adopt the processes, your awareness will improve. You'll be shocked at the magnitude of the results. Awareness is the key to beginning any process and to solving any problem. You'll notice big changes in your approach, your mindset, how you climb, and how much fun you have climbing. After you've read the book and spent some time on the rock, take this short quiz again. I believe you'll see yourself transformed.

—Arno Ilgner

Introduction

The Rock Warrior's Way is both a mental-training program and a philosophy of rock climbing that draws from the rich warrior tradition and literature. Its style is very different from what many people think of as war-like, being neither combative nor overly aggressive. Rather, it is a program of balance, harmony, and insight that is inspired by a peaceable application of ancient martial traditions. There are many books available on warriorship you might find useful. I recommend *Way of the Peaceful Warrior*, by Dan Millman, and *The Craft of the Warrior*, by Robert Spencer, as a start for anyone interested in fully exploring this rich way of thinking. *The Rock Warrior's Way* focuses on applying the warrior mindset to rock climbing, using ideas and exercises that have come from years of my own reading and research, personal experience on the rock, and work with my students in mental-training seminars.

The warrior philosophy derives from the uniquely demanding situation facing a soldier or combatant, such as a samurai, in a deadly duel. He must perform with absolute mastery and calm in the face of horrendous mortal danger. In preparation, the warrior hones his body and mind. If he does not, he will not live long. In battle, he must be acutely aware of subtle details in the environment, his behavior and his opponent's behavior, yet remain completely impassive about his own peril. If he clings too dearly to his own life, or is ruled by his Ego, he will seek escape; his attention will waver; he will be destroyed. Paradoxically, if he adopts a stance of embracing the risk and accepting the consequences, he is far more likely to survive. It is easy to see how the warrior mentality can be applied to the risky business of rock climbing.

An important component of the warrior literature for me is the work of Carlos Castaneda, who wrote of his experiences with a Yaqui Indian sorcerer don Juan Matus. Castaneda, an anthropology student, soon becomes don Juan's apprentice and undergoes many experiences in his quest for power that challenge his view of reality. Together, Castaneda and don Juan explore the warrior philosophy, which manifests itself not as a component of martial art, but in the context of adventure in nature and the mind. Castaneda's accounts of the pair's outlandish escapades in the wild, rocky highlands of northern Mexico have resonated with climbers since the books were released in the late 1960s.

The Rock Warrior's Way seeks to develop an adventurous, vigorous, deliberate approach to climbing. Initially, it breaks down the habitual and self-limiting mental framework we bring into climbing and into life in general. For most of us, when it comes to meeting challenges, our own worst enemy is ourselves. Our self-image and our self-worth are far too wrapped up in achievements. Ego controls much of our behavior. We constantly act out of fear and avoidance, rather than out of the love of challenge or of climbing itself. Our mental habits raise unnecessary barriers and often, unconsciously, drain the vitality from our performances. A major tenet of the Rock Warrior's Way is the resolution to become increasingly aware.

Therefore, much of this program involves developing awareness. We must become aware of mental processes that are subtle, taken for granted, hidden, or overlooked. We cling to what is comfortable, known, and secure—often without knowing it. Consciousness of our mental processes is the first step in understanding how they affect our performance.

I kept the text simple and free of jargon, but some warrior terminology is definitely helpful. In warrior-speak, the active form of awareness is called **attention**. Attention is awareness heightened and focused, the intentional directing of awareness. Almost everything you will learn in the Rock Warrior's Way boils down to attention and what you do with it.

Proper use of attention, in warrior-speak, is **impeccability**. Impeccability, according to the dictionary, means flawlessness. It is a word with a highly moral component. Although, in the warrior tradition, this morality is completely individual and could be described as personal integrity. In the Rock Warrior's Way, we answer only to ourselves. We take ultimate responsibility for our choices concerning what we should or should not do and what life means to us. We do this through an introspective, intuitive process that is sometimes called finding "a path with heart." Venturing out of our habitual comfort zones is essential.

When acting impeccably, a warrior directs all of his attention toward his ultimate quest: to gain self-knowledge and personal power. **Power** is another word used very specifically in the warrior tradition. It does not refer to monetary wealth or dominion over others, but rather our ability to act effectively, to venture into unknown facets of the world, to explore, and to hunt for meaning. Power manifests itself as clarity of thought and decisiveness in action. It is the totality of the resources you bring to a given situation with special emphasis on the mental aspect. Power is your level of experiential knowledge, and you increase it by expanding your comfort zone.

Essentially, a warrior is *an impeccable hunter of personal power*. He gains power by taking forays into the unknown where he focuses his attention, grapples with chaos, and learns from the experience.

The following are basic tenets of the Rock Warrior's Way mental training approach:

1. Our performance is greatly affected by the subconscious, hidden parts of our minds.

2. Improved performance occurs through a process that is fundamentally one of growth, which, in the mental sphere, we also call learning. You learn best by focusing your attention on the situation, in an attitude of problem solving.

3. Motivation is a key ingredient in performance, and the *quality* of that motivation, not just its *quantity*, matters. Performance is improved by moving away from fear-based motivation and toward love-based motivation.

4. There are two types of fear: survival and illusory. The former is healthy and helpful while the latter is not. It is important to be able to distinguish between the two fears.

5. Death is our "advisor." In other words, awareness of our mortality is a helpful reality check. It reminds us that every action matters, and thus directs our actions toward what's really important, valuable, and purpose-

ful in our lives. Death reminds us that we have no time to waste. This program is called the Rock Warrior's Way because the mental principles it uses have a close kinship with those discovered by those who were in actual martial situations. Death was so likely that unusual mental preparation was absolutely essential. Even in less perilous activities, such as rock climbing, death is still a real possibility, and this truth can help us. Ultimately, for each of us, death is certain. The question, then, is how can we use the unavoidable truth of our mortality to empower us rather than cripple and terrify us?

The Rock Warrior's Way

Learning and growth, by definition, take us out of the familiar and into the unknown. Hence, we must leave our comfort zone. Leaving the comfort zone is a risk—either real or perceived. The Rock Warrior's Way is in many ways a structure to guide risk-taking. Risk-taking has three phases: preparation, transition, and action.

The conscious mind is the primary agent active in the preparation phase. It lays the groundwork to allow the subconscious mind to effectively guide action later, when you're actually in action, when there's little time for thought. In the preparation phase, ideas and concepts are the important elements. You will "clean house" in your brain, assess, and plan. You'll learn to avoid traps such as wishing behavior. You will train to focus not on how difficult the climbing is, but rather on what possibilities are open to you. You also will prepare the conscious mind to stay out of the way once you're in the heat of action. The preparation phase includes Processes 1 through 4 below.

The transition phase, Process 5, is short: it's the moment of truth, of choice. Your goal will be to make a powerful, abrupt, and complete transition from preparation into action.

In the action phase, Processes 6 and 7, your goal is to live fully within the challenge rather than try to escape it. You'll avoid the "fight-or-flight" mentality and embrace the effort as an opportunity for learning. You will keep your conscious mind quiet, thereby allowing your intuitive abilities to come forward. You'll keep your focus on the journey, not on the destination.

Outline of the Program: the Seven Processes

1. **Becoming Conscious**. In the first process, you improve observation skills to become more self-aware. You direct awareness onto your inner dialogue. You examine the grounds of your self-worth. You detect gross attention leaks.

2. **Life is Subtle**. Attention is collected and centered. You direct awareness onto sensations in the body (breathing, posture, etc). You speak to yourself deliberately, rather than listening to the regular chatter of the inner dialogue.

3. **Accepting Responsibility**. Here, you focus on being responsible for the situation, rather than assigning blame, wishing that the situation was otherwise, or hoping for magical deliverance. Blaming, wishing, and hoping take power out of your hands. Accepting responsibility comes to terms with the objective information you gather about the risk.

4. **Giving**. Here you adopt an attitude of power: you ask what you can give to the performance, rather than what you might receive if you "succeed." You focus your attention on options and possibilities. This process collects the subjective information about the risk and comes to terms with it.

5. **Choices**. This is the transition phase, the moment of truth. You choose either to direct attention away from the risk or into the risk. Declining to take the risk is not failure. Many, many risks are foolish and taking them could kill you. The key to the warrior Choices process is to be absolutely decisive. If you're going to back off, you do it without misgiving. If you go forward, you do so with your full being, without looking back. You set an intention to act with unbending intent, which produces 100-percent commitment.

6. **Listening**. This process guides you as you act out the risk. It helps you stay on course, in the risk, rather than falling into a control mentality that will divert attention and rob you of power. You are in action now, in the unknown; you need to learn something. "Listening" to the situation and the route facilitates the learning process. This is a very intuitive process. In Choices, you accepted the possible outcomes of your effort and made the leap; now you must trust in the process.

7. **The Journey**. Once in the chaos of risk, you focus on the journey, not the destination. When you're stressed, you are tempted to rush through the stress. Yet, if you have prepared well, this stressful situation is exactly why you came here in the first place. It holds the rhyme and reason for your climbing. When you're stressed, you are in prime territory for learning. A journey mentality helps you align your attention forward into the climbing process instead of letting attention wander to the destination, or to self-limiting thoughts that won't help you solve the problem and learn.

Chapter 1
Becoming Conscious

The first Rock Warrior process, Becoming Conscious, lays the mental groundwork upon which the other processes will build. Becoming Conscious revolves around developing your powers of self-observation and examining self-limiting aspects in your current ways of thinking and acting. If you are unaware of how you think and where your motivation comes from, you have very little power to change. Without change, there is no improvement.

Your goal is to replace lazy, habitual, self-limiting ways of thinking with a disciplined mental outlook that will maximize performance. In order to make this replacement, you must gain a conscious awareness of the way you are now. In Becoming Conscious, the main task is simply to become aware that self-limiting thought processes exist and explore the how and why of them. You will identify different ways in which you squander attention and personal power, including power sinks, which funnel attention into ego and self-image, and power leaks, which fritter away attention through negative self-talk or wishing behavior.

As climbers, we think of ourselves as adventurous people, yet we often react to challenges in unadventurous ways. After we've been climbing for a while, we tend to lose the open-mindedness and quick learning that characterized our early climbing experiences. We fall into patterns and habits that limit our learning. When faced with a challenge, we become distracted from the immediate situation and fall into some sort of ego game or useless inner dialogue. We tend to be highly goal-oriented, and arriving at a performance plateau saps our motivation. Without even noticing, we become involved in an unconscious, repetitive, habitual spiral, and our power declines.

The ordinary person's mindset is one of vast unconsciousness. He is imprisoned by habit and doesn't even know it. An average person has approximately 60,000 thoughts each day, and most of these thoughts are the same ones he had the day before. The warrior's task is to free the conscious mind of this habitual thought, to direct attention more deliberately, and to respond spontaneously and non-habitually to challenging situations. Full attention and spontaneity are the keys to power, and the first step in improving those qualities is shedding light on our dim unconscious realms.

An important component of our unconsciousness is our habitual system of beliefs and motivation. Our early learning—our socialization into our culture—has determined much of the mental structure that subdues our potential.

You can feel pretty worthless at times because reward and punishment have molded you. When you did something that was considered good by your caregivers, you were rewarded, and when you did something that was considered bad, you were punished. Your caregivers associated your worth with your performance—your behavior. Then, as you grew older, your caregivers' expectations became embodied in the Ego, which took over the job of rewarding and punishing. Your caregivers' expectations were supplemented or replaced by the expectations of society at large, the expectations of a peer group, or the expectations established by a set of beliefs you adopted with little critical thought. Regardless of the source of the Ego's expectations, the result is the same: we are slaves to externally derived influences, rather than being the masters of our internal, mental environments.

We generally have adopted established beliefs rather than formulating our own. Society, of course, encourages such conformist behavior. We may be competitive or compassionate, radical or politically correct, sport climbers or trad climbers. These orientations too often derive from a deep unconscious attempt to align ourselves with people we admire or to get others to like or admire us. Though we may hold these beliefs close to our hearts, they do not come from our hearts. They come instead from that insidious mental monster called the Ego.

The Ego is a mental entity, a crude and ruthless ghost masquerading as our "self." It is a mental construct, produced by socialization, which rewards and punishes us with feelings of self-worth. The Ego lives by comparison. It identifies with events in our past—our personal history—and then compares our history to the histories of others. This comparison leaves us feeling better than or worse than, but not equal to, others.

Naturally, the Ego wants to make us think we are better than others. Yet, making us feel inferior is just as much a tool of the Ego as feeling superior. If the Ego feels we don't measure up, it will punish us, but at the same time, it will separate itself from our failing and somehow shirk the blame. It will fabricate justifications regarding why we have fallen short. The Ego may not always be able to pretend outright superiority, but it has plenty of tricks to ensure its dominance even amid feelings of inferiority. Substantial amounts of energy and attention go into the petty maintenance of the Ego. Not only is valuable attention wasted, but the whole process creates a state of separation from reality. Consequently, performance suffers.

Many discussions of the Ego appear in the books of Carlos Castaneda, and I'll refer to these books many times. In his first few books, Castaneda, a graduate student in California, describes his experiences with don Juan Matus. Although Castaneda originally sought out don Juan during an anthropological study of medicinal plants, his relationship with the old Indian quickly turned into an apprenticeship. Much of this apprenticeship involved don Juan breaking Castaneda's old habits of thought and perception, and freeing him from his Ego. The Ego's games are so plentiful and powerful that don Juan calls the Ego the "1000-headed dragon." I find this to be a very helpful image.

In order to reclaim the energy that the Ego wastes, we must usurp its power and dethrone it. In exchange for the Ego, we call upon the Higher Self. The Higher Self isn't competitive, defensive, or conniving, as the Ego is. It sees through such petty ploys. The Higher Self derives self-worth not from comparison with others, but from an internal focus that is based on valuing growth and learning. As you advance along the path of warriorship, you will increasingly replace Ego-based behavior with behavior that is under the guidance of the Higher Self.

The development of my personal Ego is not unusual. While growing up I was conditioned to believe, "I am an Ilgner and that's special." My great grandfather Paul owned a huge vegetable and fruit processing company in Germany in the early 1900s, and was a multi-millionaire. His son, my grandfather Gerhard, was an accomplished pianist who traveled the world. After World War II, the family fortune was lost, but my father, Harry, having grown up in a rich household, still saw himself as different and "better than." He was talented in several water sports including skiing, skating, sailing, and swimming. The sense of superiority came from both sides of my family. My mother's mother, Vania, was a prominent opera singer in Europe, and my mother, Kornelia, was a very talented

artist. All through my childhood, I perceived an Ilgner as "better." We didn't do things like everyone else and there was a pervasive sense of being superior.

Even as I became an adult, this flawed thinking continued. Local climbers considered me to be a bold climber who put up scary routes, which fed my sense of superiority. Ironically, there were long stretches of time when I felt inferior. I was caught in an external value system which forced me to see myself as either better than or worse than others. I compared my externals to the externals of others, concocting weak schemes why I was more or less valuable than someone else. These justifications led away from understanding and seeing the interconnectedness of the world.

Everyone can recall certain moments that leave lasting grooves in the gray matter. One such moment revealed how asinine I could act when driven by my Ego. I had just gotten out of the Army in 1980, having served in Korea during peacetime. I was driving through town with some friends late at night when the truck in front of us stopped suddenly—seemingly intentionally. I was sure the driver was purposely wanting to aggravate us, and I reacted by getting out of the car and angrily confronting him. Unintimidated, the truck driver also got out. I was fuming, but my emotions were muddled. I felt offended that the driver had intentionally stopped in front of us. The feeling was strong because I felt important for having recently served my country. Huffing and puffing I shouted, "How dare you stop like that! I just got back from Korea serving my country!" His response left me feeling like an idiot, a feeling that remains vivid to this day. "Well, I served my country in Vietnam," he stated. My Ego's comparative game had been decisively turned against me. Serving in peacetime Korea was clearly no match for serving in Vietnam during a war. I just stood there embarrassed in front of my friends. My Ego wanted some kind of response to retain its superiority, but fortunately I was finished, for the time being, with obeying its dictates. I at least was aware my Ego had made a fool of me and that I didn't want to feed it with any more stupid acts.

Don Juan tells Castaneda that if you live by the Ego, then you can count on being offended or defensive for the rest of your life. You will constantly be tricked and trapped into doing idiotic things and wasting power. It took me until age 35 to go beyond the idea that I was better than others. I also realized we are interdependent, and each of us has a value which is not determined by comparison.

Climbing on the Whitesides Headwall, western North Carolina. The route is called *The Warrior's Way. Photo: Jeff Achey*

Achievement

Once in place in our young psyches, the Ego serves as a tool of society. We are easily trained to equate our self-worth with our achievements, whether those be the traditional achievements of mainstream culture, such as wealth and "success," or the equivalent elements in climbing, such as the highest number grade or biggest mountain we have managed to climb. We have been conditioned to believe that great accomplishments somehow make us more valuable. It may be true that success in business makes us valuable to the nation's economy. It is inaccurate to compare a high-volume producer/consumer with an actualized human being. What about our true self-worth? Is our essential value as a person defined by our potential to generate cash or, for that matter, to climb difficult rock? Obviously it is not.

Achievement, as a primary motivating factor, is a self-limiting trap. Our value systems have been shaped to equate our own deepest sense of personal worth with achievement, but the light of logic casts serious doubts on this mindset. Is a poorly educated or disadvantaged person intrinsically less valuable than a business executive? Does climbing 5.13 make us more valuable than an acquaintance who merely climbs 5.11? Few of us would answer yes when the question is put bluntly. Yet, this system is deeply programmed into the average person, and it controls his sense of self-worth. The more we think about it, the more misguided a pure achievement-orientated value system becomes.

A warrior is a realist. He realizes that, in an absolute and external sense, he is no more and no less valuable than any other human being. Outside factors, such as other people's opinions, change capriciously in response to complex agendas. They are not reliable sources of self-worth because they are here one day and gone the next. A warrior knows that the functional, day-to-day value of life and of acts must be decided personally, internally.

The point is, a value structure tied to the Ego is an unconscious habit, logically flawed, and is out of tune with reality and our own natures. Ironically, not only is this value structure flawed, but it actually damages our ability to achieve those goals on which it is based, in our case, specifically, the goal of climbing harder and better.

We face a paradox. We want to climb harder in part because of our desire to achieve. Yet achievement-motivation is tainted by the ploys of the Ego. In reality, it is the good feelings associated with achievement that inspire us. We will embark upon a process of striving indirectly for the external goals we may have. The Rock Warrior's Way begins with breaking down our habitual, achievement-oriented mindset and placing our motivation on more solid footing.

Breaking Habits

Our habitual mindset feels comfortable, since it is familiar, but it draws from a shallow well. Once you carefully examine your adopted beliefs and achievement-oriented self-worth, their power begins to dry up. They lack the heart and the force that accompanies a true inner guidance system. One of the warrior's first tasks is to establish an internal value structure that taps into deeper reservoirs of motivation. This structure will increase the power available to respond to challenges, in climbing or in any other aspect of life.

Developing a new, internal value structure requires increased awareness, but the process of becoming aware feels threatening. New beliefs and new ways of thinking—by definition—threaten the comfort zone we build around ourselves through familiarity. This comfort zone is complex and full of defenses. It is composed not only of self-limiting habits, but of unconscious mechanisms designed to protect those habits from the harsh light of objective self-examination.

Habits protect themselves by staying hidden or unconscious, but once noticed, their cover is blown. We begin to feel foolish for indulging in them. Once we're aware and suspicious of them, self-limiting ways of being cease to be unconscious habits that produce automatic—and often negative—results and responses. They become part of consciousness, subject to revision and change. The mental energy that old habits once required is liberated, and the components of the old value structure become raw material for a new and powerful mindset.

Prepare yourself to be challenged and to be uncomfortable as you read further. If these words have struck a chord within you, you have already embarked on the process of Becoming Conscious.

The Witness

As with all the Rock Warrior processes, the key step in Becoming Conscious is to focus attention. In this case, you focus attention on your inner self, on the flow of your own thoughts. Sit back for a minute and let your mind wander. You may be thinking of a hard climb you haven't been able to redpoint, which is what led you to pick up this book. Soon your thoughts drift off to what you'd like to have for lunch. Maybe the image of a person pops into your head, or a random memory of something that happened last week. There seems to be no logic or order to these thoughts. They simply pass through your head like a movie, apparently out of your control. The point is not how these thoughts come about or what they might mean. Rather, you can stand back and watch them. They are not you. When you "stand back" like this you have done something important; you have located the **Witness** position.

By identifying the Witness position and going there, you separate yourself from the complex goings-on within your conscious mind that affect your life and climbing performance. This separation allows you the objectivity necessary to analyze and change habitual or unconscious ways of being. It also provides the sense of autonomy necessary to examine issues that threaten your Ego, such as, how you develop your self-image and assign your self-worth. Knowing there is an inner you independent of any beliefs or thoughts gives you the power to change.

As the Witness position creates a place for you to conduct your observations, it also effects the thoughts and feelings you're observing. By itself, it will not reverse self-limiting thoughts, but it does help these thoughts be less overwhelming. In 1985 I was going through a divorce and was overwhelmed with feelings of negativity. One winter night during this time I was driving with my mother through the country. A full moon reflected off sparkling snow that had just fallen. As we were driving, I was feeling bitter, angry, and resentful. All of my attention was focused on these negative states. My mother noticed my state and asked why I had to be so sad and angry. "You don't even see the beauty of this winter evening," she said. She was right, and her comment stirred the Witness in me. I noticed my sour attitude, the beauty of the evening, and my resistance to letting go of the unpleasant mood in which I was immersed. Even though I wasn't able to let go of my negative thinking, I noticed it and knew that I wanted to let it go. My awareness was piqued, and it was the beginning of the transformation of my attitude.

Performance, Self-Image, and Self-Worth

Self-worth is how valuable we feel. Self-image is our sense of who we are and what we can do. Self-image directly affects how we perform. Regardless of our actual level of fitness, if we feel strong, agile, and adventurous, then we climb better than if we feel weak, clumsy, and meek. Climbing hard—and "hard" is always relative—involves making moves that feel improbable, and continuing when the situation seems nearly hopeless. If you have a low opinion of yourself, you will have difficulty imagining yourself doing the unlikely things necessary to make it through your climb. If you can't imagine yourself doing these things, you won't do them. You absolutely must have an image of yourself as one who is capable of pulling it off. All the training in the world will have minimal benefit to you if you don't give yourself *room to believe*.

Unfortunately, you can't simply improve your self-image on a whim. You need to uncover the roots of your self-image and value system and reshape the hidden structure holding you back. Fortunately, this detective work doesn't require an advance degree in psychology. The typical person's self-image suffers partly from its attachment to past performances, which anchor us more than they need to, and partly from an externally derived sense of self-worth, which poisons motivation.

Mentally speaking, past performance should function as a platform from which to move ahead, not as a limit on what we might accomplish. The strength of our arms and fingers is the most noticeable factor that affects climbing performance, but we put far too much stock in it. Some people climb at a standard far above ours with far less strength. When a climber runs out of strength, it's usually because of the strength he's wasted, not from an essential lack.

Think about your best performances. Chances are the essential difference between these and others was something in your mind—a mysterious, unexplained confidence, or a feeling of joy from being in an inspiring setting. Your outstanding performance probably was in some essential way simpler than your normal performances. You had less clutter in your mind, better focus, and fewer cares. This is typical. Performance is most easily improved not by adding things, but by removing obstacles. Maybe the difference was an ironic but common one. You felt a complete lack of performance anxiety specifically because you were out of shape and had no stressful expectations to cloud your efforts. Think of a time when your mental state made all the difference, and use that as a proof and reminder that on any given day, you can exceed your past performances without being physically stronger.

Our self-image shapes our day-to-day performances, dulling them down to what we consider "normal." This concept of normal is essentially a habit. The most significant factor that differentiate top climbers from the rest of us is their habitual sense of "normal" performance is extraordinarily high. They may approach a 5.12 or 5.13 climb with the conviction that they will not find it difficult. This mindset, this self-image, goes a long way in creating that reality. The expert expects to find a way to climb through the hard sections so he quickly homes in on that way. He expects to be able to rest, and he finds rest positions. We, on the other hand, home in on the difficulties, the obstacles, and the certainty that we will become exhausted. The expert knows there may be difficult moves, but is confident he will find a way, and that he has enough reserve for a climb of this difficulty. We balk at the hard moves because we fear we won't make it unless we do them exactly right. We fear the moves will exhaust our reserves, and we won't be able to cope with what follows. These are mental habits produced by our image of our abilities. This image, not our lack of strength or technique, is our most limiting factor.

Part of Becoming Conscious is to recognize that our self-image is not an objective description of our selves or our immediate capability. We can experiment with new attitudes, new self-images. We've experienced the expert's mindset, even though we may have only mustered it for a climb rated 5.2. Our performances are constantly being sabotaged because we cling to a self-limiting self-image based on past performance. If you can fully embrace the new belief that your mind, not some external factor, is limiting you, then you open up powerful possibilities. You begin to hoist the anchor of your past performances.

Habitual self-image is one limiting factor you can work on. Working on self-image involves redefining yourself. Another limiting factor is self-worth. Working on self-worth involves changing what you value. Our self-worth constantly becomes tied up in our performance. If we want to improve, we need to test ourselves on challenging climbs, but a diet of challenging climbs will yield plenty of performances that fall short of our aspirations. Poor performances can make us feel like "failures."

Many people lose effectiveness in their climbing (and other aspects of life) by tying their self-worth to how they are performing. All of us have experienced this to some degree at some time, and many of us feel it constantly. If we are climbing well, we feel good, not just about our climbing but about ourselves. After a "good" day on the crags, we might be confident, upbeat, and self-assured in all our affairs for days afterwards. Conversely, a "bad" day can make us feel down and unsure not just about our climbing but even our jobs, relationships, or our optimism for future happiness. In short, climbing rewards or punishes us, as if we were naïve children and climbing was our parent.

Babysitting your self-image or hunting for personal power—climbing can be either, and the choice is yours. *Photo: Jeff Achey*

Basing your self-worth on climbing performance puts you at the whim of external factors. These factors may be random and misleading. Comparison is one source of illusion. Perhaps you felt that you performed well on a certain climb because your partner was having an off day and found the climbing very difficult. You found it only slightly difficult and conclude that you were climbing quite well, when in fact you were climbing no better than usual. Or, your partner was at the top of his game. You felt lame in comparison, when in fact, objectively, you put in a very strong performance. Environmental factors may be involved. Perhaps you mastered your day's objective due to especially favorable conditions, such as low humidity, when in fact, you really didn't climb particularly well. In all these cases, the good or bad feelings you have are not based on something you can take credit for. If the performances boost your self-worth, the boost is grounded in fiction.

Perhaps you truly did climb well. You rose to the challenge and applied your skills admirably. You can, then, honestly derive satisfaction from the effort, but beyond that, what else? Should your self-worth get wrapped up in the event? Are you a better person for having accomplished your climb?

No. Authentic self-worth comes from an internal value system, not from simple achievement. Self-worth comes from the positive results of your effort. You may have learned something about yourself or gained the experiential confidence to attempt more difficult challenges. These effects are genuinely valuable. The achievement itself, however, is no reason for an elevated sense of self-worth. You might not have learned anything from your "success," or you could have learned something equally valuable by not meeting your objective.

Here's the complete scenario for performance-oriented self-worth: If you have a string of weak performances, you'll be down on yourself in general, creating a destructive downward spiral. If you climb well half the time, you'll be the passive recipient of reward half the time, and of punishment the other half. If you manage to climb well all the time, you'll get the dubious reward of becoming an egomaniac with a precarious self-image, destined for a crash. You can look forward to an old age spent in endless rehash of past days of glory. If you think about it, no matter how well you climb, tangling up your self-worth with your performance is a lose-lose situation.

Instead of simply falling into this habitual self-worth mindset, analyze it. Focus your attention on it. Discover its logic, or lack thereof. In the light of consciousness, its hold on you will begin to break down. You will see that external achievement is not the root of anything really valuable that we can derive from a climbing challenge. So what is? What can we take away and really use?

The answer: learning. Hard climbs push us out of our comfort zone, and once in the unknown, we can learn. Often, in the midst of the challenge, we push ourselves in ways we didn't know possible, gaining knowledge that we can't lose. And, if our effort is strong and creative, we can gain that knowledge regardless of the outcome of the climb. Achievement may or may not be the result of an effort, but the essential payoff of the experience is learning.

An important principle of Becoming Conscious, then, is to untangle your self-worth from your performance. You will perform better on some days than on others for reasons ranging from muscle fitness at a crucial instant, to the temperature of the rock, or to what music you listened to while driving to the crag. This should not be a self-worth issue. Achievements are satisfying, but simply having them doesn't increase your personal power, regardless of what your Ego may tell you. If you want a more consistent and authentic source from which to draw a sense of self-worth and personal power, you will eventually need to reject external factors such as comparison and achievement. You must look inside and embrace learning.

Learning to Love and Loving to Learn

Let's recap the process so far. I've said that many climbers are largely unconscious of how they think about their climbing, and of how they attain their sense of self-worth. All of us fall prey to hidden, habitual thought patterns that lead to sub-optimal performance. Indeed, these thought patterns and performances comprise our sense of who we are. Yet, the Witness position reminds us we are not these things. We are not our thoughts, but the observers of those thoughts. Once we consciously appreciate the Witness position, our mind becomes a field of inquiry. We observe that our thoughts about self-worth are tied to achievement. We also identify that this system of thought is flawed. We realize that it promotes performance plateaus and general unhappiness. Our habitual thought system is stubborn, but once we're aware of it and dissatisfied, we begin to look for a better system.

When you focus on the external outcome of your efforts, you are at the mercy of chance. You worry about making it up your climb, and how you'll feel if you don't. If things go your way and you make it, you'll react to the outcome with happiness. If things don't go your way and you don't make it, you'll be unhappy. Either way, you are reacting to a situation that is out of your control—a stressful, unempowering state of affairs.

If, on the other hand, the self-worth you derive from your climbing is based on what you learn during the experience, then you are less concerned about the outcome of your efforts and able to focus more on the effort itself. What really matters when facing a challenge? What matters is learning. You want to test yourself, throw yourself into something outside your comfort zone and see what you're capable of. Your true goal is not to conquer fifty feet of inanimate rock, but to expand your abilities through learning.

With a focus on learning, awareness improves. During the climb, you're free from anxiety and therefore, free to apply yourself more fully to the effort. Obviously, this mindset increases your chance of making it up your climb. After the climb, your thoughts focus on the internal process, not the outcome. If you fall off your climb, you are not plagued by thoughts of failure. You don't kick the rock and yell, "I suck!" as some climbers do, nor quietly hang your head, victim-like, and let your performance affirm a poor self-image. Instead, your attention goes to the positive aspects of the experience: what you learned, what mistakes you made, why you fell off, what you will do next time in the light of your new knowledge. Self-worth does not enter the picture. Your self-worth comes from inside, from your dedication to the quest for knowledge, from a love of learning. This gives you a more realistic and consistent basis for your motivation to climb and improve.

Of course, shifting over completely to internal motivation is easier said than done. Most of us have a combination of internal and external factors motivating us. To increase the power of your internal motivation and reduce your dependence on external factors, it helps to analyze what's important to you and what you're passionate about. Spend some time identifying the things you love about climbing. These may include the beauty of the rock and environment, the friends and companionship, and the many complex factors that relate to challenge and achievement. Beauty, friendship—these are ever-present in climbing. Our experience is improved by taking the time to appreciate them, and to remember that whatever happens, we are involved in these things we value. The last category, challenge and achievement, requires more careful analysis.

Do you love to challenge and test yourself on a difficult climb, or do you simply love the feeling of accomplishment or the praise from your peers once the climb is over? If love of praise and need for gratification are your core values in climbing, you are drawing from a shallow well. If you could be forever surrounded by weak, inept climbers, who constantly fed your Ego, would you choose that, even if it meant that you never improved? Would the pleasure and satisfaction last? Would you knowingly choose such a situation over one where your Ego had to struggle face-to-face with climbers more accomplished than you?

The Ego plays a game, making arbitrary rules so that it can win. If it's losing, it makes excuses and creates a fantasy world where it could have or should have won. The tricks of the Ego are not helpful or meaningful ways of thinking. Rather, they are traps that we all fall into when we become separated from what we truly value. Connecting with the deeper reasons you climb is essential for progressing in the Rock Warrior's Way.

Looked at objectively, your self-worth is essentially static: you are worth the same as anyone else, no more and no less. Having made it up climb X, Y, or Z is not relevant. You may be glad to have accomplished these climbs, but they have not increased your worth as a person. Yet your best climbs have given you something. You can feel it. What is it, if not self-worth? It is growth. The experiences have helped teach you something about yourself. They have increased your self-knowledge and thus your personal power. Once you learn to consciously separate achievement from self-worth, you become free of the self-limiting need to establish external "proof" of self-worth. You're better able to focus on what the efforts of climbing really can do: improve the self through growth and learning. For most climbers, a little soul-searching will go along way toward replacing the value of achievement with the value of learning.

Shifting from external toward internal motivation gives *you* the power to determine value and worth. Thus, internal motivation builds self-confidence. Variable external factors play a smaller role in how you feel about yourself. You are in tune with what you are doing, with your strengths and weaknesses, and you have a reliable, stable core to your being. You are not invincible, but your abilities can be counted on. This is confidence—confidence in your self. Self-confidence gives consistency to your performance. By having a solid core, you're more comfortable and secure in the uncomfortable, insecure atmosphere of a climbing challenge. This core grows when you value the learning above the achievement.

Power

The ability to do things, the ability to learn, having energy to apply to new situations, self-confidence, boldness—all these are elements of something the warrior literature calls **power**. We are not speaking here of conventional power, control over others through money or influence, but rather something more personal. Power is the ultimate goal of the warrior. Doing difficult climbs, taking risks, challenging oneself, doing new things—these are undertaken for the purpose of increasing personal power. For the Rock Warrior, power is the currency of climbing effort. It appears in the form of full attention, shrewd analysis, timely action, inventiveness, explosive effort, and commitment. Power gets the job done and transports the warrior into the wild and risky places where opportunities for learning abound. Above all else, a warrior is a hunter of personal power. He takes proper care of the power he has and constantly searches for more.

Power Sinks

We all have generous helpings of personal power, but we waste it. One form of waste is called a **power sink**. Power sinks are energy-sapping elements of our personalities. The first power sink is *self-importance*. In an ordinary frame of mind, we constantly sink attention into unconscious, ineffective, Ego-promoting thoughts. The Ego's sense of self-worth, as we have said, relies on petty comparison, being better than or worse than others. A warrior, in contrast, sees self-worth as a non-issue. He is equal to others. He doesn't sink power into proving to himself that he is as good or better than others. Instead, he is aware of the self-importance power sink and stops it. Instead of valuing a personal identity relative to others, he values learning, growth, and situations that increase his personal power.

The second power sink is generated by the Ego and involves self-image. The Ego goes to great pains to maintain the fiction of a constant, unchangeable self. This is a manifestation of the Ego's hunger for security. Just as the Ego likes to brag about its achievements, showing it is better than others and thus worthy of value and survival, it likes to cling to the past and create a complex, detailed identity out of past events. The warrior literature calls this element of the Ego, *personal history.* Identification with personal history creates this power sink.

At face value, personal history seems benign, yet perhaps you can sense its power-sapping ability. Do you feel threatened by me calling your personal history a hindrance? If you do, then your Ego is raising one of its thousand heads.

Personal history is comprised of your fond memories, great triumphs, and saddest days, all claimed by and attributed to an essentially unchanged you. These highlights add to the richness of our experience, but they come

Whitesides, North Carolina. *Photo: Jeff Achey*

with excess baggage. Many elements of personal history are not landmark moments in our lives, but rather oft-repeated, self-limiting ways of being, frozen at some early stage of learning. These fossilized responses are the habitual you. The maintenance of a fixed self-image requires energy. We are constantly and sometimes strenuously reframing new experiences to fit our old concept of ourselves. This requires power that could be directed towards facing challenges in the present.

One simple example of excess baggage is my own climbing experiences on Whitesides Mountain in North Carolina. Early in my climbing career, I made several first ascents on what's known as the Headwall of the 700-foot face of Whitesides. It was a very intimidating section of cliff, unclimbed before my first ascent, and locally was considered impossible. Doing first ascents on this unclimbed cliff made me feel important. My Ego filed away those experiences, identified with them, and looked for ways to inform the world that I was more "important" than others. "I'm important," said my Ego, "because I'm a bold climber who did the first ascent of the Whitesides Headwall." That's my personal history. That personal history makes me feel special and separate from others. Separation, however, leads away from learning and understanding.

So how does that personal history affect me when I climb in the present? If others are watching me climb, I tend to worry that I won't live up to the bold image I've identified myself with. I end up shunting energy trying to maintain an image, when I should be using that energy for problem-solving on the climb. These positive and satisfying experiences in my past have become a power sink because I haven't been able to release my Ego's sense of personal history. Many climbers I know have similar difficulties. They feel nervous climbing in front of others. They can't fall or people will "know" they aren't as good as their reputation makes them out to be.

A more general example of personal history could be poor footwork. Perhaps your past is full of experiences of popping off small holds, banging your knees, and making unnecessarily strenuous moves to avoid relying on your feet. This is how you see yourself; it's part of your personal history. Whether you realize it or not, part of your sense of self comes from having poor footwork, and therefore, the Ego puts energy into maintaining that aspect of your self-image. Though the Ego may chastise you for it, it wants you to have poor footwork, giving itself an excuse for not climbing harder. The power sink of personal history binds you to your past in an endless, energy-sapping feedback loop.

The warrior can't tolerate such a waste of power. He is much too deliberate with his energy and attention. He doesn't waste power on boosting his self-importance or maintaining a fixed self-image. In fact, he actively attacks the devices of the Ego in order to free attention for use in the challenges of the present. When he's climbing, he channels all his attention toward problem-solving within the challenge.

Power Leaks

Power sinks drain personal power into mental activities such as bolstering the Ego and maintaining a fixed self-image. Another way to lose power is to fritter it away in ineffective mental habits, limiting self-talk, reactionary behavior, or hoping and wishing behavior. We call this category of power-sappers **power leaks**.

The first power leak is ineffective mental *habits*, things we do automatically with no conscious involvement. Certain habits adversely effect climbing performance. One example is placing too much protection on a trad climb—too much meaning more than is needed to keep you safe and provide reasonable back-up for pieces that might pull out. You might do this even though the effort you expend to place protection causes you to fall.

Consider the habit of chalking your hands. Some climbers spend so much time nervously chalking their hands that they lose the ability to climb smoothly and continuously. As you become more conscious of your climbing habits you can begin to analyze them and discard the ones that inhibit your performance.

The second power leak, intertwined with habits, is *inner dialogue*. Your inner dialogue is the voice inside your head that seems to accompany and advise you when you're facing a challenge. Most climbers' inner dialogue, however, is not an effective climbing coach. Instead, its function is to reinforce habits.

For example, when faced with a difficult move, the voice inside your head might say, "I don't trust my pro." You may then react by not pushing yourself to the point of falling. If the pro really is untrustworthy, the voice is legitimate. But too often, the voice derives from a more complex agenda. The details vary, but you may recognize this unhelpful mental game. You react to the voice by placing more pro, thus using up so much energy that you give yourself an excuse for not climbing. You slump onto your gear, claiming (to yourself or your partner) that you got pumped because the pro was so strenuous to place. In fact, you had solid pro at your knee, but you were listening to a habitual inner dialogue. You really did trust your pro, but your Ego wanted to hide an embarrassing fear—the unjustified fear of having to risk an obviously safe fall. Placing unnecessary gear allowed you to get too pumped to move past the pro you had placed, thus eliminating a real leader fall. Your effort, however, was sabotaged.

A second form of limiting self-talk happens after the climb. It seeks to fossilize your recent behavior into a permanent aspect of your self. We touched on this earlier when we discussed identifying ourselves with our performance. After taking a long time to lead a pitch, it may be accurate to say, "I climbed slowly." It is a great leap, however, and not a logical one, to say, "I am a slow climber." As objective observers, we may analyze our climbing performance and conclude, "I gave in, gave up, and let go." It is incorrect and self-limiting, however, to turn this into an absolute, and say, "I give up when it gets hard." Yet this is a mistake we often make. A warrior takes responsibility for each time he gives up. To talk as if giving up was a permanent personality trait is simply a power leak.

Inner dialogue tends to be self-limiting. If you can't silence it, then you will be a slave to it, doomed to act out those self-limiting thoughts. You will have difficulty learning, since your inner dialogue reinforces your previous state of unconsciousness. Your perception stays fixed in its original position, unaware of any options. When you diminish inner dialogue you become silent, and possibilities open up. Switching off that nagging inner voice takes time and practice, and we'll return to it later. The first step in the process is simply to become conscious of your limiting self-talk.

The third power leak is *reacting*—emotionally and rigidly—to an unwanted event. You react when you receive an outcome different than what you wanted or expected. Let's say you didn't want to fall off a climb, but you did. You react by becoming angry and kicking the rock. Why? Chances are, you don't know why you're upset. You are reacting unconsciously to a scenario of self-worth set up by an external Ego orientation. The Ego surrounds itself with external rules such as "falling is failing," or "5.10 should be easy." If your Ego is in control of the situation, you will react when these externals are threatened. The Ego's security and identity is threatened, so you become defensive and react.

The key to stopping reacting behavior is awareness. You can practice awareness on the rock or at home. Personally, I have a greater tendency to react, to get offended or defensive, when I'm feeling weak, agitated, anxious, or powerless. One day when I came home from work feeling agitated, I reminded myself that I would have a tendency to react rigidly, possibly lashing out with harsh words. Sure enough, when I entered my home, my children were loud, hanging all over me, wanting to play, and asking questions. Knowing that I was prone to reacting, I was prepared. I was able to breathe, relax, and watch myself in a detached way. I played a short time with my children and then told them I needed time alone. I had prevented a power-draining reaction and felt good about the encounter, even though I was feeling agitated and in need of quiet.

The fourth power leak is *hoping and wishing* behavior. Hoping and wishing are passive states. If you hope a situation will turn out the way you want, you're passively waiting for external influences to determine the outcome. You aren't thinking actively about what you need to do to achieve what you want. "I hope I redpoint this climb" is worse than passive. It has a negative effect. By indulging in passive mental processes that don't help create the outcome you want, you are actively leaking away power that could otherwise be applied to the challenge at hand.

Wishing is also passive and leaks away power. "I wish this hold was more positive" has no action quality to it. By wishing, you try to decrease your discomfort by escaping into a fantasy. This is a dreadful waste of power. Not only do you have power going into passive behavior, but you also cloud reality, impairing your ability to problem-solve. Remember that learning is the warrior's goal. The holds are what they are. You need

Stressful, high-standard traditional climbing, as found on this route in Eldorado Canyon, Colorado, provides many opportunities for growth. *Photo: Jeff Achey*

to think actively so that deliberate, effective actions follow. Instead of wasting power by wishing the hold was more positive, use that power to determine how to use the hold in the best way possible.

Becoming the Observer

To become conscious, you need to separate yourself from the experiences of your life. Become the observer of these experiences and a critic of your responses. You are stalking personal power, and the first step is to become aware of how you respond to life's circumstances. Too often, we react automatically, in accordance with powerful, self-limiting habits that are resistant to change. We would like to be able to snap our fingers and have all self-limiting habits disappear, but we're not wired that way. We need to become conscious, and then proceed with patience, intelligence, and stealth.

One way to deal with negative self-talk is simply to *delay*. I experienced the power of delaying quite vividly in 1996 when I teamed up with a friend, Glenn Ritter, to climb the famous and difficult *Astroman* route in Yosemite Valley. As we climbed through the initial pitches I wasn't feeling very confident. Each pitch tested me, and I experienced a continuous stream of negative self-talk: I couldn't finish the climb, the Harding Slot pitch would be too hard, this long and sustained climb was too big a challenge, the exposure was too great, etc. By the end of the fourth pitch I wanted to go down. Instead of acting on my negative thoughts, however, I simply watched them from the Witness position. I didn't really do anything, like fight the thoughts or chastise myself for lack of boldness. I simply listened quietly to the negative self-talk but delayed acting it out. After the fifth pitch I began to feel more confident. The limiting self-talk dissipated. I noticed that I was climbing well, and had been all day. I stayed receptive to the situation, continued climbing, and completed a fantastic and very challenging route. Best of all, I learned something.

Delaying is especially helpful when dealing with habits. Imagine that you are halfway up a strenuous sport route, climbing with some difficulty and not very smoothly. You find yourself getting progressively more pumped. Forty feet up you make it to a bolt, feeling very uncomfortable in the effort. You clip in and now that you can relax a bit, at this island of safety, the self-limiting talk begins. "Take!" The word wants to jump out of your mouth. Your arms hurt and a shrill voice is telling you that you need to escape the discomfort—now! Do you?

You don't. In fact, you have a great opportunity. A habit is formed by associating one thing, such as your arms feeling too pumped to continue, with another thing, such as yelling "Take!" If you break the automatic association, then you begin destroying the habit.

Don't do anything. Don't react to the insistent, comfort-seeking self-talk. Instead, simply observe yourself. Listen to the self-talk. Listen to your conscious mind squirm in the discomfort of being pumped, but don't act. Be the Witness. If you really are pumped, you won't be able to continue the observation session for long. It doesn't matter. A few seconds is enough for you to begin breaking the chain of association. You have proven to yourself that you don't have to say "take" when you're stressed out and pumped. It's not an automatic response. You have options, and delaying gives you time to consider them.

Delay is the first step. The next is to *dissociate* from your habitual response. In dissociating, you separate yourself from your performance. Here you are working against your habitual self-image as a person who gets pumped and then yells, "Take!" Instead, call attention to yourself as an autonomous person, capable of making new choices. Call yourself by name, and give a different command not derived from your habitual response to discomfort. Faced with the above scenario, I might say, "Okay Arno, even though you think you're too pumped, just climb into this next section anyway, since the fall won't be that long." If you can do this—delay your response and replace a habit with a fresh action—then you've accomplished a powerful feat.

Another classic scenario for habitual reaction occurs after a fall. You might habitually react in one of several ways. Maybe you get upset and frightened by the feeling of the fall and react by giving up and going down to the ground before examining your options. Maybe you're self-critical and react by saying something that turns your performance into an absolute, such as, "I'm worthless at this kind of climbing!" Or maybe you react with anger and charge back up without spending any time analyzing your fall or considering what you might do to change your approach.

Next time you fall, observe your reaction. Your goal is simply to develop awareness, to catch yourself when you react, and to stop that reaction.

Becoming Conscious is a process that improves awareness, develops an empowering self-image, increases self-confidence, and builds personal power. You accomplish this not by striving directly for an empowering self-image or self-confidence, as goals, but simply by shifting attention inward. Your goal is to gain awareness—to learn—and thus to gain access to deeper and more powerful sources of motivation. The 1000-headed dragon of the Ego has a thousand self-limiting ways of reacting to stress and protecting itself, and many of these ways have become habitual and unconscious. Thus, the Ego is your constant foe but also your teacher. As you gain understanding, you will be able to collect more personal power by diverting attention away from power sinks, such as self-importance, and plugging power leaks, such as wishing or reacting.

Once we cease to be defined by our past performances and achievements, we begin to see ourselves less rigidly, and as full of potential. Our newly liberated power is ready to be put to use. The next day climbing we might see a complete change in the way we are able to use our minds and bodies on the rock. No matter how our performance turns out, we have the chance to experience profound learning from the fresh material provided by our efforts. All that's required is that we pay attention. The action word for Becoming Conscious is **Observe**. Use this word to remind yourself of the elements in this chapter.

Chapter 2
Life is Subtle

In Becoming Conscious, you unraveled the devices of the Ego, channeling attention away from power sinks and plugging power leaks. That process frees attention—power—that previously was unavailable to apply to your climbing. In the Life is Subtle process, you collect and center that attention.

Climbing is full of subtleties, and we constantly overlook them. Take, for example, balance and poise. Intellectually, we understand that these are important elements of technique, yet we constantly botch the subtleties. Here's a typical scenario: A climber arrives, fairly pumped, at a clipping stance on a sport climb. He is ten feet out from his last bolt and very anxious to get clipped in. He's tense, over-gripping, and out of balance. Gritting his teeth, close to falling, he finally makes the clip—and instantly relaxes. Immediately he finds another good handhold within reach. A sloping foothold he mistrusted suddenly feels very adequate. He shifts body position slightly and finds he can stand at the clipping stance almost effortlessly. Before he clipped the bolt, he felt he could pump out and pitch off at any instant. After clipping, he was at ease. The stance was the same, but his use of it was quite different.

Does this sound familiar? It is ironic that we are least likely to demonstrate poise in the situations that demand it the most. Our climber most desperately wanted to be balanced and poised when he was ten feet above protection, not when he was safely protected by the bolt. Yet, his attention strayed to the possible fall and to his anxiety over that fall. He did not notice the subtleties in the rock that would have allowed him to be completely comfortable before clipping. All he could see was his goal: clipping the bolt. He did not notice the subtle

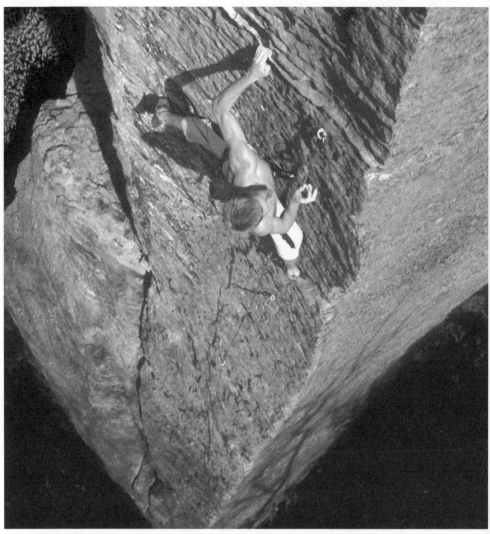

Stretching to clip bolts too soon is energy wasting and fear based. Focus on efficiency and climb to the most advantageous stance to make the clip, as this climber has done in Kentucky's Red River Gorge. *Photo: Shullphoto*

flaws in his technique that were rapidly draining his strength and throwing his body out of balance.

A friend of mine experienced the importance of subtleties during the first free ascent of a very difficult climb called *Fiddler on the Roof* in Fremont Canyon, Wyoming. The crux of the route involves climbing a ten-foot horizontal roof. Steve Petro, a very strong climber, had worked out the sequence of moves in two halves. The first half involved five feet of upside-down finger jamming, and the second involved long moves between assorted flakes and hand jams. Steve had worked the route for many months, and though he found the moves very difficult, he was consistently able to climb either half of the roof. But despite strong efforts, he couldn't link the two halves of his sequence into an all-free ascent. Even when he felt strong going into the second section, the linkage thwarted him—again and again.

Frustrated, Steve finally gave up his claim on the project and offered the first ascent to Todd Skinner, who was traveling through town. The pair went to the route and Todd suggested that Steve give it another go. Steve got on the route and, again, could climb both halves separately but couldn't link them.

Todd went up and worked the moves out the roof. Then he came down and gave Steve a subtle suggestion. Todd, a very precise technician, had noticed something while Steve was climbing. Steve kept body tension through each half of the climb, but when he transitioned between the two halves of his sequence, his hips sagged down slightly. Todd felt that if Steve would suck in his hips during the transition he would be able to link the sequences. Steve took Todd's suggestion, and on his next effort linked the two halves and made the free ascent. *Fiddler on the Roof* is rated hard 5.13, but we really don't know how hard it is because no one has repeated it. Todd couldn't do it, nor could other climbers who gave it their best efforts. The difference between the free ascent and countless efforts involved a three-inch shift in the position of the hips.

Petro's subtle hip shift was manifested by his body, yet its root was in his mind. By breaking up the climb into sections, a useful tactic, Steve was able to focus on and refine two more manageable sequences of moves. Steve's body, intuitively, knew how to keep the hips tight to the rock when moving from jam to jam. The transition between the halves, however, formed a psychological break, a place where Steve had not applied his attention. As his mind jumped from the first sequence to the second, the flow was lost, hips sagged, and that brief loss of attention was enough to sabotage the ascent.

There are two points here. First, little things matter. The attention you pay to the chance of a fall, rather than to maintaining poise, drains large amounts of energy. The way you perceive a climb, the body memories you develop as you work a sequence, the words you choose when you speak to yourself—everything you do, no matter how subtle, has an impact. The Life is Subtle process is about learning to notice the little things and using attention to perform them impeccably.

The second point is that the body and the mind are a single, interrelated unit. The body has characteristics that we normally think of as

belonging to the mind. Your body has "memories," which sports physiologists call schemas. (Schemas are referred to as engrams in Europe, but schema is the accepted term for American physiologists.) Schemas allow you to "remember" the complex combination of muscle activity and balance involved in riding a bicycle. Schemas exist partly in your brain and partly in the nerves and fibers of your muscles. Steve Petro developed specific schemas for the two halves of his roof climb, but he didn't develop an efficient body memory for the mental gap between the halves. We could say that Steve's hips sagged down through that mental gap. Just as there is no clear separation between brain and nerves, there is none between body and mind. The whole thing works as a unit, the *bodymind*.

Poise

A key element of creating a supportive, high-performance bodymind is poise. Poise can be broken down into three components: body, including your posture and facial expression; breathing, which serves to integrate the bodymind; and mind, which includes internal behavior such as, how you speak to yourself.

Physical Posture—the Body

Dan Millman, in his audiotape program *Everyday Enlightenment*, says proper posture is a way of "blending with gravity." You want to position your body so you're in harmony with your environment. Poor posture wastes power. It takes extra energy and attention to hold the body when it's out of balance. If the body isn't balanced perfectly along the spine, then muscles are using energy to hold it. Proper posture uses minimal energy to hold the body upright. Posture has mental effects, too. When you stand with proper posture, you appear more confident. This is no mere appearance. The more you explore the workings of the bodymind, the more you realize that appearances count. Proper posture actually gives you a sense of confidence. Body language sends messages not just outward to others, but inward, to you.

Proper posture says you own the space you occupy, no more and no less. You aren't cowering and apologizing for the space you're using, nor are you jutting out aggressively into space you don't need. You own your space not because you're better than others, but because you see yourself

Steve Petro nearing the transition point on his route *Fiddler on the Roof*, Fremont Canyon, Wyoming. *Photo: Beth Wald*

on equal footing with others. You say, "Right now I occupy this space and it is mine. I have a right to be here, in this space." This kind of mindset keeps the Ego in check, and it's just the kind of mindset you want when entering into a climbing challenge.

Proper posture, incidentally, opens your chest cavity and enhances the quality of your breathing. It places you in a position of alertness and readiness for action. Use proper posture and poise while standing and climbing. Stand in balance, straighten the back, bring the hips in and shoulders back, open the chest. Do you feel it? This body positioning brings with it a sense of confidence. Stop using poor climbing posture, such as body positions that have a cowering or cocky feel to them. Find a balance. The subtleties of posture will determine what kind of body you take into the risk process.

Your face is another important component of poise. Your face is both a passive indicator of how you feel about the state of affairs in the body-mind and an active control center for the bodymind. If you have facial expressions of doubt, then the bodymind is doubting. Adopt a look of confidence, and a sense of confidence builds in the bodymind.

Many climbers grimace during strenuous parts of a climb. Grimacing is a stereotypical response to pain or discomfort, and it is more than just a response. It can magnify or create these feelings. Climbers often grimace during exertion, but exertion need not be painful or uncomfortable. If you grimace during exertion, you cast a mood over your effort that triggers specific reactions in the bodymind. Grimacing is defensive, a form of recoil. When you grimace you contract the skin around your eyes, reducing your peripheral vision. Grimacing also sends an analogous message to the mind; it creates tunnel vision, limiting what you can mentally "see," such as creative new possibilities. A grimacing face creates a mindset that is ready to tough it out in the trenches or to escape, not one ready to openly and creatively embrace the challenge.

Instead of allowing your face to grimace, deliberately keep the face relaxed with a "soft-eyes" focus. Eyes should be comfortably open, held softly, not squinting or staring. Your attention should be on the whole field of view rather than on specific points in that field. Don't focus on your hands, your feet, or one portion of the rock. Rather, spread out attention and look at color, depth, shadows, and the interrelationships between objects.

A discussion of soft-eyes focus appears in Castaneda's book *Tales of Power*. Don Juan states that, when used properly, the eyes can detect an enormous number of features including details that are too fleeting for

Your face not only expresses your state of mind—it can create it. A relaxed face (below) leads to relaxed, efficient climbing. A tense, grimacing face (right) creates extra stress and may exaggerate your perception of difficulty.
Photos: Shullphoto

normal vision. The eyes pick out subtle details that would be missed if they were focused too narrowly on one feature at a time. Also, says don Juan, by not focusing on specific things in your field of view and by paying attention to everything, you encourage a quiet, receptive mind, rather than one preoccupied with the distracting internal chatter about the particular things being perceived.

In the preparation phase, soft-eyes focus gives you relaxed facial poise and helps you gather as much information as possible. Just as our habitual thought patterns can get in the way of our seeing a situation in a receptive way, so too, our habitual ways of physically looking can make us blind to many features of the world. In the action phase, soft-eyes focus will help minimize the involvement of the conscious mind, thereby diminishing the internal dialogue that tends to take over when you're under stress.

Integration of the Bodymind—Breathing

Breathing connects the body and mind. It is the only bodily function that can be totally voluntary or totally involuntary—totally conscious or totally unconscious. As a result, breathing works in two directions. Your unconscious breathing expresses the state of your bodymind. Conscious breathing influences that state. Breathing, therefore, is a powerful tool that you can use to gain control in stressful situations.

When you are stressed, your breathing has an automatic tendency to become shallow and erratic. You may even hold your breath, which further stresses the bodymind system. Stress tends to produce poor breathing, and poor breathing increases stress. It's a feedback loop that can ruin your composure and hinder your performance. Deep, regular breathing, on the other hand, can reduce stress.

Pay attention to your breathing as you prepare yourself to enter a climbing risk. Is it shallow, rapid, noisy, or irregular? If so, make a conscious effort to breathe more deeply, slowly, quietly, and continuously.

Proper breathing may take some practice. Take a minute to notice the subtleties of how you breathe. Simply relax and breathe normally. Put one hand on your chest and one on your belly. Does the chest or the belly expand as you breathe? Where is the breath? The next time you are on a climb, see if you hold your breath. Holding the breath is a common problem among climbers.

As you become more aware of your breathing, you can begin to influence it. Typically stressful breathing takes place high in the chest. When you're relaxed, the diaphragm should move down when you inhale, pushing the belly out slightly. This is called belly breathing. Belly breathing automatically slows down the breathing cycle because the inhale/exhale process takes longer. Belly breathe continuously and give equal attention to the inhale and the exhale. Proper breathing immediately sends the message to the subconscious that all is well, and that you are in control.

Proper breathing:

- Dissipates fear, stress, and anxiety.
- Brings your attention back into your body and the situation facing you.
- Oxygenates the blood, reducing lactic acid and carbon dioxide.
- Keeps primary blood flow going to the muscles, rather than shunting it to the internal organs.
- Integrates you—connects the body, the conscious mind, and the subconscious mind.

Two exercises will help you gain better awareness of your breathing:

- Complete Exhalation. People generally breathe too shallowly. The purpose of this exercise is to bring the breath deeper into the belly. Take a deep breath and then exhale. Without inhaling, exhale even more, until you cannot exhale any more air. The inhalation will then happen automatically, and the breath will expand into the belly. Doing this exercise several times will create a more complete breath.

- Deliberate Breathing. As you climb, simply focus on breathing continuously. With each breath force the air out with your abdominal muscles. This causes the inhalation to be automatic and the breath cycle to be longer and deeper. I also like to hear the exhalation by blowing the air out of my mouth. Doing this indicates to me that I am breathing continuously.

Mental Posture—the Mind

In the Becoming Conscious process we discussed the ploys of the Ego, how we can stalk it and understand its power over us. We discussed the comparative, externally oriented value system that lies at the root of the Ego's power, and proposed an alternative, internal system that values learning and growth. In the Life is Subtle process, we refine this internal value system and begin to apply it. Doing this reclaims the power wasted by the Ego.

Deep belly breathing can help relax and center you. *Photo: Shullphoto*

Why do you seek out a challenging climb? Climbing achievements matter little in the grand scheme of things. They don't create world peace, send your children through college, or even make you a "better" person. The learning that can take place in the process of your climbing achievements is what matters. Climbing can challenge you to the core, which is valuable and allows you to learn about yourself and expand your possibilities. You dig deep on a climb, gain self-knowledge, and apply that self-knowledge—that power—to any situation. If a climb you expected to be difficult proves to be easy and doesn't challenge you, then it loses most of its benefit. Remember the importance of feeling challenged. Once in the thick of things on a climb, we quickly forget why we are there.

In addition to being mindful of your motivation for climbing challenging routes, it's also important to give yourself room to learn. This involves keeping an open mind about your abilities and your perceptions of the difficulties you're facing. You may think of yourself as "a 5.9 climber." On the surface this sounds like a simple description, but too often it is a hindrance and a rigid belief. Many "5.9 climbers" I've worked with quickly find they are capable of doing 5.10 climbs simply by letting go of their firm belief that these climbs are too hard for them.

Learning and growing is a process of modifying your beliefs. If you're too attached to your beliefs, you won't be willing to modify them. When you identify yourself with your beliefs you become attached to them. Without realizing it, you become defensive when they are threatened. You feel personally threatened. In Becoming Conscious, we introduced the idea that your beliefs are not you. Be mindful of that. Don't let unconscious feelings of self-preservation make you cling to limiting beliefs.

Efficient learning requires an open mind. To be open-minded means you don't cast out new information before evaluating it, and if it's useful, making an honest attempt to incorporate it into your present way of thinking. But beware! Few people actually admit to being or feeling close-minded. The Ego doesn't allow that. We trick ourselves into thinking we are objective and open, when in fact we may be judgmental and closed. Once again, the mind is full of subtle tricks. We monitor our open-mindedness and our motivation when we pay attention to the content of our self-talk.

Our thoughts take the form of words. We speak to ourselves, from one part of our conscious mind to another. If this internal dialogue wasn't so common, we might think it quite odd; different parts inside us are discussing and debating issues. Such internal dialogue involves, by definition, a lack of integration of our entire bodymind. In times of concerted action, we will seek to turn off this dialogue debating mechanism completely. When we're assessing a risk or preparing for action, however, we can make use of this dialogue by taking conscious control of its content.

In his book *The Fourth Dimension*, Paul Cho states that the speech center in the brain rules over the nerves. Your nerves influence your body and physical actions. For this reason, limiting self-talk can waste vast amounts of attention and power. If you speak in self-limiting ways, your actions will

be limited. If you speak in empowering ways, however, your actions will be empowered. There are four specific methods you can use when speaking to influence your actions. These methods create deliberate speech.

To speak deliberately:

• Express a possibility attitude.
• Use power words that are active, not passive.
• Direct your words in an efficient direction.
• Speak in questions.

First, express a possibility attitude. The self-talk that occurs in your head will contain clues about the attitude you have unconsciously adopted. Talking to yourself consciously can also create a different attitude. If you say, for example, "My arms are too short for that reach," you've essentially declared the move impossible. Without a doubt, this attitude will result in you feeling the move to be impossible. However, if your attitude is, "This is possible," your bodymind orients itself positively to the situation, seeing it as a challenge to be mastered. If you consciously say, "What could I do to make that reach?" you've implied the move is possible and have given yourself options. Make sure your self-talk embodies an attitude of possibility. By expressing an attitude of possibility, you retain your power to act in the situation.

Second, use power words. Use words that retain power and keep you active.

Here's one example of how a performance question and the resulting answers can be greatly influenced by the words you use in framing it. Listed below are a student's answers from a written exercise involving the words *problem*, *challenge*, and *opportunity*.

Question 1: "What is your biggest *problem* in improving your performance?" Answer: "My biggest problem is being afraid of falling."

Here, the student's fear of falling is not related to any action. The answer orients the student passively, stuck in an unconscious attitude of avoidance of falling.

Question 2: "What is your biggest *challenge* in improving your performance?" Answer: "My biggest challenge is figuring out how to deal with falling."

Warrior posture: hips in, weight over the feet, face relaxed, mind focused on actions to take, not the difficulties faced. Photo: Shullphoto

This is more helpful. Figuring out how to deal with falling is more action-oriented and has an element of seeking to engage the fear and to work through it.

Question 3: "What is your biggest *opportunity* in improving your performance?" Answer: "My biggest opportunity is to practice falling so I won't be afraid of it and can enjoy climbing more."

Now the student has a plan. She has indicated a specific action she can take, and she also stated a strong motivating reason to engage her fear— to enjoy climbing more.

Third, speak actively, in a direction where positive results can occur. Passive or reversed self-talk is common. A simple example is, "Don't forget your keys." Here, you tell yourself not to do something that you don't want to do in the first place. Subconsciously, this is confusing and inefficient. It saps attention. You introduce the idea of forgetting your keys, and then direct yourself to prevent this from happening. It's more direct to say, "Remember your keys." The word "remember" moves you directly toward what you want to happen. "Don't fall" is similar in structure to "Don't forget your keys." It is better to say to yourself, "Stay in balance," or "Keep moving." If you're focused on moving and staying in balance, there is little mental space for worrying about falling or actually falling. Your attention is on doing something empowering, not on avoiding something limiting.

Fourth, when facing an obstacle, speak to yourself in questions rather than statements. Statements leave you no options. They are either true or false. If you are in the midst of a climbing challenge, you don't know if your statement is true or false. Stating, "This fall is too dangerous," leaves you passive. You're not assessing how dangerous the fall really is, and what you might do to mitigate the danger. Questions, on the other hand, offer new information to consider and sends a demand to your subconscious to supply options. An alternative way might be to ask, "How dangerous is a fall?" and "How can I make a fall safer?" These questions keep you involved in the problem-solving process.

Power Words

Some words simply don't work for the warrior. We tend to use words habitually, without thinking about what they mean. Internally, however, we know what they mean, and we unconsciously respond to the words. Some words are unnecessarily passive. Other words are "loaded" in one way or another. Many words we use are habitual "figures of speech" that may have hidden meaning. Actions follow the words we use. To act deliberately, we must speak deliberately. Doing this helps retain and utilize power impeccably.

Words to stop using include *success* and *failure*. Success and failure label your performance in a way that devalues the learning process. When you climb you produce an effort. That effort has an outcome. Rather than label the outcome as success or failure, focus on your actions, on what helped and what you might change next time.

Good and *bad* are loaded words. Typically, they represent oversimplified judgments based on unconscious values. An easy example is "good" or "bad" weather. Rain may be "bad" to a climber who wants to go climbing but to the local farmer, it may be "good." Is rain good or bad? Obviously it's neither. Rain is simply rain. When describing wet weather, stick to the facts and describe the rain. If it's you who fell from the sky, don't call it a "bad" performance. Simply describe the performance.

Another word that a warrior doesn't use is *worry*. Worry is a passive form of fear, which comes from an old Anglo-Saxon word meaning "to choke or struggle." You don't want to choke or struggle. So don't worry. Be actively concerned. Better yet, be curious.

People typically use the phrase "take care" or "be careful." These focus on being guarded and cautious instead of staying receptive to the situation. Being cautious is passive. If there is danger in the situation, you need to actively pay attention to enhance your ability to respond. A warrior isn't careful; he is observant and he pays attention. In his book *Psycho Cybernetics*, Maxwell Maltz sums this thought up with, "Don't be too careful."

People often say, "I have to," when referring to a task they dislike. "I *have to* work full time," implies that you have absolutely no choice. In fact, you *choose* to work. Working produces income for things you've decided are important, such as food or your children's college tuition. You could also choose to quit work and accept the consequences. The point is, it's your choice. You're in charge. By using the habitual phrase, however, you create a fictional reality where nothing is your fault. You pretend to be the passive victim of circumstances that conveniently excuse you from responsibility. You might turn down an invitation to dinner by saying, "I have to study." In fact, you choose to study, but you don't want to say that because you feel it will hurt the host's feelings. The deception can become quite complicated. After a weak performance on a climb, you might say in disgust, "I have to start training!" What does this mean? It doesn't mean very much, really. You're pretending to scold yourself. It's a dishonest way to obscure the situation, to twist the words and shirk responsibility. It's a way to avoid saying, "I *choose* to start training."

A warrior doesn't use the word *try*. Steve Petro likes to say, "Trying is lying." Try has an element of vagueness that gives you an excuse. It implies that you might not make it, and if you don't it really won't be your fault. "Trying" means that you're unconsciously focusing on unknown factors that might prevent you from reaching your goal.

When you speak in this vague way you place a verbal limit on your power. You willingly give away power to a mysterious something outside of your control. In fact, there will be numerous ways to improve your effort that were overlooked. That is the challenge: to notice these subtle details and act instantaneously with power, not simply to try. Do not hold yourself to the habitual old standard of mental effort.

Instead of saying he'll try, a warrior states he'll do it. His intention is to give his best effort, but he doesn't put a limit on that effort. He knows he's not perfect and he may not make it. The difference is he knows it's not helpful to emphasize this possibility with a power-draining word like try. For him, doing the climb essentially means engaging the process; the outcome is less important. When people say try, they are thinking of the outcome instead of the process of learning. A warrior doesn't try because he's focusing on his effort, and effort is something applied, not tried.

Center Yourself

The Becoming Conscious process helps you be aware of the many sources of power within you, and the many ways you waste that power. Life is Subtle is about taking that self-knowledge and consciously shaping your bodymind into a more efficient, powerful unit. The way we stand, the expression on our faces, how we breathe, and how we talk to ourselves—all these contain subtle opportunities to gather or waste power. The little things are immensely important. Dan Millman councils us that "every act is a deliberate act of will. Even when tying your shoes—tie them impeccably."

When faced with a climbing challenge, collect and center all available attention within you. Guide your self-talk into channels of power. Take a deep breath, exhale strongly, and shake your face to get rid of any grimace. Push your hips in close to the rock and bring your shoulders back. The action word for the Life is Subtle process is **Center**. This word will remind you of the essence of this chapter and help you focus attention as a warrior.

Chapter 3
Accepting Responsibility

The third warrior process is Accepting Responsibility. So far, you have plugged power sinks and power leaks in order to retain attention. You have collected and centered your attention within you to make it available for the climbing challenge. In Accepting Responsibility, you will use your attention—your power—to cut through delusions and misconceptions in the situation facing you, replacing them with useful facts and an empowered approach. You will use your developing warrior mind to become aware of pitfalls that can sabotage your performance and to direct your attention actively on what will enhance it.

There are strong influences in our society that discourage us from accepting responsibility. We expect every intersection in town to have a stop sign and every trail hazard on a ski run to be marked. Our courts are full of lawsuits that seek to blame wet floors or hot coffee for causing injuries that are clearly the result of our own inattention. We have made it the job of our government to enact laws requiring us to wear seatbelts. All of these things fuel our habitual tendency to blame others for our own mistakes. Slowly but surely, we develop the unconscious conviction that our own safety is someone else's responsibility. Climbing, by its nature, tends to counteract this socializing influence, but most of us continue to bear its mark.

Ego, too, plays a role in our shirking of responsibility. The Ego is constantly equating our self-worth with our achievements and performances. We have an innate need to feel good about ourselves. When our Ego is in charge, we tend to protect ourselves by transferring responsibility for a poor performance to someone or something else. The Ego is shrewd and will try to appear objective and rational when it blames, but its logic serves a single goal: boosting an externally derived self-image. This defensive tactic saps our power to respond effectively to challenges.

The Ego is careful not to reveal its machinations too easily. It knows how to pick its battles. Thus, most of us accept responsibility for things we have obviously brought upon ourselves, especially if these things don't seriously threaten the Ego. If we drink too much one night, we probably can accept responsibility for the hangover the next morning (although even then we might try to blame it on the cheap wine). If we drop and break a plate, most of us can accept responsibility for the blunder. If, however, the cause of the event is less direct, the situation more complicated, or the event more personally threatening, then we often fall into some form of non-acceptance behavior.

Suppose you severely sprain an ankle while playing basketball on your lunch break at work. It's right at the beginning of the spring climbing season, and you had been training hard for an upcoming climbing trip. Now, you'll be on crutches for six weeks. This feels like a terrible stroke of bad luck, a real injustice. You spend hours at a time wishing that the injury hadn't happened. You blame "stupid ball sports" for causing the injury. You even secretly blame your co-workers for persuading you to play basketball. You mope around, brood, and feel sorry for yourself. Throughout this process, you are draining away power.

You would be better served by an active mindset, where you claim control over as much of the situation as possible. You chose to play basketball, and you got injured. Those are the facts. Wishing that you weren't injured doesn't help. Blaming the uneven basketball court or your co-workers simply drains away attention that you might otherwise direct toward a tangible benefit, such as analyzing mistakes in your lay-up technique, or choice of footwear, and seeking out an aggressive rehab program.

Even if your injury is more serious and the cause further out of your control, a position of choice and power is still available to you. Maybe you were blindsided by a drunk driver. Choosing not to accept responsibility for your situation keeps your attention focused on blaming and wishing, rendering you passive and impotent. Your attention is spent on things that can't be changed, making that attention unavailable to work through your rehabilitation. The well-known climbers Eric Weihenmayer, who is blind, and Mark Wellman, who is paraplegic, are excellent counter-examples to the passive, blaming, wishing mindset. They have chosen to see their "misfortunes" as challenges which allow them to gain a fantastic sense of learning and accomplishment. They have gained far more in personal power than they ever lost through their physical setbacks.

Many years ago when I lived in Wyoming and climbed frequently in Fremont Canyon, I had an interesting experience concerning the power of accepting a situation as it is. Steve Petro and I were working on making the second ascent of a crack route called *Morning Sickness*. The first ascent had been snatched away from us locals by Mark Wilford and Skip Guerin, two talented climbers who had visited from Colorado in 1983. Steve and I were eager to do the second ascent to see if we could match the skills of the visitors.

The route was quite difficult and started about ten feet above the water of the North Platte River. It began with a five-foot roof and then continued vertically to the top. Surmounting the roof required a reach past the roof to a shallow jam. I could just barely make the reach, and moving on from there repeatedly thwarted me. Steve, being two inches shorter than me, had even more trouble reaching the jam. In fact, he kept complaining about being too short to make the reach. We worked on the route on several visits, and each time Steve would complain about being too short.

Finally I got sick of his excuses, and more out of annoyance than warrior wisdom, I told him to quit complaining and accept how tall he was. I told him he wasn't going to grow any taller and the roof wasn't going to get any shorter. The next time we went to the route, we both made it. Years later he told me I had really shocked him by what I had said. My remarks woke him up to his shirking-responsibility behavior and allowed him to accept the situation as it was. When he quit wasting attention on complaining and focused directly on the challenge, his whole approach changed. He quickly figured out exactly what rock features were available to work with and applied himself fully to using those as best he could—which was all it took.

Top-level performances occur when this sort of reality check is in effect. Sometimes our climbing seems effortless and we climb with great focus; other times we may struggle and whine. We finally get mad at ourselves, drop our excuses, and improve our focus in that reactive sort of way. The anger that comes with that approach, however, is extra baggage. The art is to maintain a calm and empowered attitude when a challenge requires time and/or effort. Lynn Hill summed up her attitude nicely in her video about her first free ascent of *The Nose* of El Capitan and the prolonged and intense training program she was engaged in. She made several epic attempts on the route, each of which was very costly in time and effort: "Throughout the months of preparation, I practiced an attitude of acceptance. No matter what the situation, I made an effort to remain patient and relaxed each step of the way."

Reach, don't whine. *Photo: Shullphoto*

Shirking and Accepting

The two worst enemies of Accepting Responsibility are detachment from reality and passive thinking. Wishing behavior ("I wish these holds were bigger," "I wish I was taller") embodies both. We dream up an alternative reality of bigger holds and longer arms, and channel our attention into that fantasy. The attention going into the fantasy is unavailable for doing anything active, such as figuring out how best to use the holds that exist. Hoping is as passive as wishing, with the difference being that instead of conjuring our own fantasy world, we channel attention into waiting for a favorable world to be created for us. When we say, "I hope I make it up this climb," we embark on the effort passively. We delude ourselves that some external power, rather than the pure quality of our effort, will determine the outcome. We wait for lucky breaks instead of working skillfully toward our goal.

The most passive of all delusions is victim thinking. We pretend that so much misfortune has befallen us that we can no longer be held responsible for taking charge of our lives and improving our situations. The victim mentality can be so obvious that it appears comical to an outside observer. We can all probably think of examples of our own or friends' "poor me" behavior. This mentality also can be subtle. For example, some trad climbers I know harbor murky excuses that relate to why they haven't excelled at sport climbing. They resist pushing themselves to the point of falling. When questioned, they may finally admit, in so many words: "I'm a trad climber who was taught that 'the leader must not fall,' so there's no way I can be expected to get comfortable taking falls." In fact, this is a ploy of the Ego claiming to be a victim, when in fact, it is merely clinging to a comfortable but limiting old habit. Certainly there are situations, such as very runout trad routes, where a fall will cause injury. I'm not referring to routes like this. Making a blanket statement, however, that a leader must not fall limits us and causes us to stay stuck in an old habit.

The trad climber may further obscure his sport-climbing and falling issues with moral overtones. In fact, the whole concept of accepting responsibility is often morally charged. The warrior, however, does not think of accepting responsibility as a moral issue. The warrior's concerns are pragmatic, and "right" and "wrong" are inappropriate concepts for the job. By not accepting the maximum amount of responsibility we reduce our ability to respond and therefore our power. Learning how to respond to tough challenges in a way that increases power is one of a warrior's most important tasks.

Describing Objectively

An important component of the Accepting Responsibility process is gathering objective information. Objectivity, however, can be surprisingly elusive. Our expectations cause us to lose our objectivity.

The ultimate model of objective inquiry is scientific research. The scientist, a trained observer, carefully examines factual data, formulates ideas, and conducts experiments to rigorously test those ideas. What could be more objective? Even in the "hardest" sciences, however, expectations and associations seem to influence the results. In the early research of quantum physics, for example, scientists attempted to determine whether light was essentially made up of particles or of waves. Some scientists designed experiments to detect wave-like characteristics, such as interference, while other experiments were designed with particle behavior in mind. Each kind of experiment found what it set out to find. Light eventually proved to be a more mysterious entity that possessed *both* wave and particle characteristics, but this outcome at first hadn't been considered possible. Even in science, then, the expectations associated with an inquiry can undermine pure objectivity.

In our own inquiries, objectivity is even more slippery. We often unconsciously lie to ourselves. In his book *The Gift of Fear*, Gavin de Becker relates a relevant story about expectation and self-deceit. A man was home alone and heard a noise downstairs. He went to check it out, telling himself, as many of us might, that he was "making sure everything was okay."

"Making sure everything was okay," however, was not an objective description. In fact, it distorted the task. The man heard a noise and his intuition linked that noise to danger. Being honest with himself about that danger, however, would have been too frightening. He obscured the danger by pretending that he was going downstairs simply to verify safety.

The man's unconscious attempt to control his fear gave him an expectation that interfered with his ability to perceive the situation as it really was. Instead of conducting his search with the expectation of finding danger, the man searched with the expectation of finding nothing. This interfered with his ability to take proper precautions and deal wisely with what he discovered—an intruder!

Fear is one cause of poor objectivity, but self-deception can derive from sources other than fear. Justification is another scheme for lying to yourself.

An example might be a person pilfering postage stamps from his company. This is an apparently insignificant act, but it's the structure of the justification, not the magnitude of the offense, that makes it interesting to analyze. The stamp-pilferer holds the view that stealing is wrong. Since he holds that view, he can't admit to himself that he is actually stealing the stamps. He says to himself he is underpaid and the company owes him at least a few inexpensive stamps. Or, he says to himself that his personal correspondence in some way benefits the company.

Most of us participate in some sort of justification scheme like this to excuse ourselves from the rigors of our supposed beliefs. The average person is quite creative with the little justifications he can think up to deceive himself that his actions are not out of line with his purported beliefs. If we confront ourselves point blank with our words and actions, however, we know that we are lying. Scrupulous honesty is required to realize this. Removing small lies from our day-to-day life cleanses the whole system. If you stop lying to yourself about postage stamps, you stop lying to yourself about climbing, why you aren't stretching, or why you turned the lead over to your partner. You come to grips with reality, and reality is a more effective teacher than illusion.

Tricking yourself is similar to lying, but you do it consciously. I've heard and read about climbers advocating that you trick yourself into believing you can do something. Even if this tactic achieves some short-term benefit, it's a fool's approach.

If you are on a runout route, preparing to do the crux, and tell yourself, "There is a bolt right at my face," you are intentionally creating a make-believe situation. You might manage to reduce your stress level, but tricking yourself is the surest way to get yourself into risks that aren't appropriate, nor ultimately valuable. The Rock Warrior's goal isn't to get up a certain climb by hook or crook. It's to gain personal power. He gains that power by taking forays into the unknown with the conscious intention of taking a risk—an appropriate risk that will allow him to learn but won't hurt or kill him. Instead of tricking yourself by creating a false, non-threatening situation, you should be giving your full attention to the real situation. Where is the last pro? Where is the next pro? How far is the potential fall? How much power do I have left? Why am I feeling hesitant or fearful? These questions enable you to learn from the situation and lead to greater understanding, growth, and power. That's the goal, not climbing the crux. You want to understand the risk—the reality of the situation—as clearly as possible. Tricking yourself works against that process.

Past experience is another source of self-deception. People constantly cloud their perceptions by looking through associations, metaphors, and memories, rather than describing things in the moment. Climbers do this all the time. When you look at a crack climb, are you filtering your perception through past experiences, or are you simply observing objectively? Let's examine the three forms of non-objectivity that can come from relying too much on past experience.

Association is linking together things in your brain. If you think of one thing, you think of the other. For example, you may associate crack climbing with pain. Does a crack climb look painful? How can something *look* painful? If you see a crack climb as painful, you are associating. Other climbers could look at the crack without thinking of pain and ascend the crack without experiencing pain. You have apparently had painful crack-climbing experiences, and you now associate cracks with pain. Separate the two components of those experiences and you can begin the process of learning how to climb cracks painlessly.

A second form of non-objectivity is *metaphor*. It is a process of abstraction, representing something to yourself in an abstract way. For example, if you see a crack as a wound, then you are thinking of the crack metaphorically. Thinking this way, you will automatically carry over the emotions you associate with wounds that don't belong to cracks in rock. There may be negative connotations attached to wounds, making cracks metaphorically repulsive to you.

Memories also can taint your objectivity. New things can remind you of a similar thing you experienced in the past. A certain crack climb—perhaps all crack climbs—might remind you of a climb called *Keyhole* at the Shawangunks, on which you struggled desperately during your first year of climbing. The memory of *Keyhole* colors your perception of all cracks, and you presently avoid crack climbs.

If you look and describe objectively, a crack is a feature on the rock face with definite contours, steeper here and less steep there, wider here and narrower there. It will admit various parts of the body and will take climbing protection such as nuts or cams. These characteristics have nothing to do with associations you have about crack climbing in general, nor with crack metaphors or memories of specific cracks in your past. Being aware of associations, metaphors, and memories can help you describe situations more objectively, and loosen the self-limiting aspects of past experience.

Responsible Climbing

Clearing your mind of the past and the subtle habits of deception helps you look with fresh eyes towards gathering useful information, to help you climb. Let's move on to gathering that information, to discerning the true nature of the challenge facing you.

Climbers suffer from a variety of flaws in their problem-solving ability. We often overreact to an unexpected challenge before we even know for sure what the challenge entails. We tend to wish a situation was different, rather than focusing on what we can do given the facts.

In order to accept responsibility for taking a risk, we need to know what we're accepting responsibility for. Too often in climbing we are under the power of *phantom fear*, a vague, nagging fear of unknown origin. There may be no real substance to such fear. Conversely, the fear may indicate real danger. However, the fear is of limited protective value unless we can identify the specific danger that's causing the fear. Often, phantom fear is simply a general fear of the unknown, of the world outside our comfort zone.

Phantom fear makes risk-taking an effort. This is beneficial, to a point, because without some resistance to risk-taking, we might be soloing 5.13s and killing ourselves. Without taking some risk, however, we can never learn anything, never expand our comfort zone and make progress. To take appropriate risks, and to take them well, we need to weaken phantom fear.

By its nature, phantom fear can't be investigated directly. It's a phantom. Phantom fear creeps in when your information about a risk is too vague, and it grows as you focus on it. You can reduce phantom fear by improving your understanding of a risk and by describing your climbing situation objectively. Be vigilant with the words you use in your description. If you say, "This section of the route has good holds, but it looks pumpy," you aren't being objective. "Good" is a value judgment about the holds. What do you mean by good? If your goal is to be challenged by the climb, good might mean the holds are small, sloping, and strenuous to use—but you probably mean the opposite. By saying "good," you color reality with ill-considered wishes and intentions.

Stick to the facts. A more objective description would be, "The holds look flat, four fingers wide, and about finger-pad deep." Remember, precise wording and radical objectivity are important. You are involved in a two-fold search for information. Some of the information you're seeking involves the rock. Just as important, you want to uncover what might be in your mind making you hesitant, inefficient, or unprepared.

Analyzing the Challenge—Risk Assessment

Analyze means to break down into parts. Taken as a whole, a climbing challenge can be overwhelming. Broken down, it becomes more manageable. When you actually launch into a climb, you'll immerse yourself in the experience as a whole. When you're preparing for a challenge, you can break it down into parts. There are three parts to the climbing situation: the route, the fall consequence, and the climber. First, there's the route, the entire route or the section you're facing, possible holds, and protection points. It's important to identify what it is about the route that will challenge you. Second, there's the fall consequence, the falls you could take from different points on the climb. Third, there's the climber (you), the skills and abilities you bring to the climb, specifically those skills and abilities that will help you deal with the challenge of the route. In the Accepting Responsibility process, we focus on clarifying these elements of the climbing challenge. We're interested in dispelling illusions and gathering all the useful facts. In the next chapter, Giving, we'll focus on using this information efficiently.

The First Part—the Route

First, assess the route. Determine what it is about the route that will challenge you. Doing this will identify which skills and abilities are most important to assess in the third part of your assessment, the climber part. The details of how you analyze a section or route will vary with the kind of challenge you've chosen. If your goal is to on-sight a sport route, you will analyze as much of the route as you can see from the ground, gathering information you can use in your effort. You'll look for key rest holds where you will have a chance to regroup, or sections that are possible cruxes. Once you begin, you may be pretty much on the run. One long assessment opportunity may be all you get. On a sparsely protected, multi-pitch traditional route, in contrast, where protection is a major issue, you will be able to see less of the climb before you begin and may climb more slowly and deliberately, and assess in sections. You might look up at the lead ahead and find the next island of safety where you are fairly confident you will find solid protection. You might back off if the route above proves too demanding or dangerous. Let's examine the more complex trad-climbing example in more detail.

You have climbed thirty feet from a belay ledge and you encounter a smooth wall. You can see a horizontal crack ten feet above where you are pretty sure you'll be able to find large holds and place gear, but the wall leading there appears dauntingly blank.

It's not blank, however. The holds and features are simply more subtle. As you assess the rock features up to the crack, you see sharp horizontal edges, there and there, smaller holds, there and here, and possible sidepull holds, here and here. After a few minutes of such inspection your "blank" wall is covered in holds. None is larger than half-inch, and some are much smaller, but all are potentially usable. You're not envisioning

Be comfortable at your stance and assess the situation. *Photo: Jeff Achey*

sequences at this point (although in practice, as you become more proficient, the Accepting Responsibility and Giving processes may blend somewhat). Your goal is simply to destroy the illusion that the wall above you is "blank." By doing this you've made major inroads into the unknown, diminishing phantom fears.

Next, assess the gear possibilities. You have a solid cam just below your feet, but you'd like to place a nice high piece right here. There is no placement, however, and the wall up to the horizontal looks crackless. No, halfway up is a thin seam that may take gear. There appear to be holds nearby that may be large enough to allow you to stop and place a piece. Gear placements include a very likely opportunity for a piece in ten feet, a questionable piece before that, and a solid cam below your feet.

OK, you've assessed the route. In practice, you may spend more time doing this, perhaps climbing up and down to feel holds and check out possible body positions. For the sake of brevity, however, and to keep our focus on the essence of the Accepting Responsibility process, let's move on to the rest of the assessment process.

The Second Part—the Fall Consequence

Second, assess the fall consequence. Your goal, again, is to see clearly what you're facing and not be overwhelmed or deceived by the challenge. "If I fall here," you say, "then I will go about eight feet onto that solid cam just below my feet. If I place my feet where my hands are now, then I'll be able to see if I can place something in the seam. If I can't make the placement and fall, then I'll go just about twenty feet with rope stretch but still land ten feet above the ledge. If I don't get gear in the seam and fall on the very last move reaching for the horizontal crack, then I could hit the ledge."

This assessment does not imply that you actually are willing to take any of these falls. That decision-making process will come later, in the Choices process. Your sole focus now is to assess the situation clearly and objectively, to take responsibility for what you're facing and not deceive yourself, hide from the facts, or overlook any useful information.

By now you have ample amounts of ammunition against phantom fear. The daunting unknown has been replaced by a very detailed idea of the challenge facing you. Perhaps you are more scared than ever. The demands are significant—a classic bodymind climbing challenge. Most climbers, however, find themselves significantly calmed by clarifying exactly what they are facing. Knowledge is power, so the saying goes, and the unknown is scarier because you have no power over it. Knowing exactly what you're facing is much safer than forging ahead blindly.

One experience that taught me not to ignore the fall consequence occurred in 1979 when I was climbing with my friend Steve Anderson at Stone Mountain in North Carolina. Stone Mountain is known for its very pure, very low-angle friction climbs, and its very long runouts. I'd climbed on Stone a year before, doing some of the harder routes without falling. After that experience I adopted the attitude of simply focusing on the climbing, giving little attention to the fall consequences. If you're confident or cocky as I was, this "go-for-it" approach comes fairly easy at Stone because you can climb quite quickly on the low-angle slabs without giving much thought to specific moves. The low-angle rock also minimizes the feeling of exposure. This approach had allowed me to climb several hard pitches until I found myself off route without an escape on a climb called *Mercury's Lead.*

I had climbed past two bolts and found myself about 100 feet up and fifty feet above my last bolt. I could see the next bolt, only ten feet up and to my left. Unknowingly, I had climbed along some edges that took me up and right away from the usual line of the route. The route was rated 5.9 but I'd climbed up a series of edges that felt more like 5.10. Now, I was poised on small foot and handholds, realizing I'd climbed into a predicament. I made a few attempts to climb left to the bolt, but the moves seemed too thin. I downclimbed a move or two, but the moves I'd made to reach that point felt too tenuous to reverse.

I was faced with a harsh realization: I would have to commit to the move or fall off. For the first time on the lead, I assessed the fall consequence. I would probably hit the tree-covered ledge where Steve was standing 100 feet below. I realized I'd climbed into a very dangerous situation without much forethought. I hadn't assessed the fall consequences at all. I hesitated for close to forty-five minutes, shaking out one leg at a time and procrastinating.

Finally I went for the moves. The edges were thin and rounded, my balance was off, I was overgripping the small handholds—and then I was off.

Soon I was skidding down the rock on my back. I noticed Steve pulling in slack. It was as if time slowed down, and he had plenty of time to pull in sufficient rope to keep me off the ledge. I was speeding faster and faster down the rock, but the rope came taut before I hit anything. I survived the fall with only some scratches on my elbow.

Had I assessed the consequences of a fall, I could have decided if the risk was acceptable, rather than having to simply accept the consequences once I found myself in trouble. I could have consulted with Steve and worked out a belay plan. I could have prepared myself by figuring out the best way to slide. Fortunately, Steve was attentive and responded instinctively by pulling in that ten feet of slack that saved my life.

In fact, unbeknownst to us, my terrifying near-miss was quite unnecessary. The more experienced Stone Mountain climbers had excellent contingency plans they used when putting up these routes. Belayers would remain unanchored so they could run down or across walls or ledges to take in many yards of rope to shorten the leader's fall. The sliding leader would stay centered over the balls of his feet and maintain balance by "patting" the wall as he slid to avoid scraping the skin off his hands.

I didn't learn these techniques until later, but right away I learned simply not thinking about the fall consequence is not a wise strategy. Falling is part of the climbing process and can happen on any route. The lesson became even more valuable when I realized the danger of the fall itself could have been greatly reduced with creative forethought and/or practice.

The Third Part—the Climber

Third, assess the climber, the skills and abilities you bring to the climb. Potentially dangerous situations are in some ways the simplest. You can determine the risk, assess it, and take responsibility for your choice. Accepting responsibility is more difficult when it involves the murky workings of the Ego, rather than real concern for life and limb.

One of the Ego's "1000 heads" arises when you examine your performance after the fact. Backing off a climb is a classic example. When you back down, even when you are sure you are making the appropriate choice, you may later begin to doubt yourself. Your Ego is still attached to the external reward of claiming a hard ascent. Even though you knew in your heart that you were showing respect for the gift of life by backing down from an overly dangerous, inappropriate risk, your Ego may not be convinced. It's scheming, and wants a trophy climb to feed its inexhaustible appetite for glory, using your shame to obtain it. The Ego, however, has only as much power as you give it. By consciously acknowledging this second-guessing as a product of the Ego, you already drain it of force. To finish the job, simply look that dragon head in the eye and slice it off.

Don't waste attention on wishing you could have performed better with "shoulda-coulda-woulda" behavior. Once you've had a performance, it's

The beautiful and thrilling slab of *Mercury's Lead*, Stone Mountain, North Carolina. Photo: Shullphoto

over. You can't change it. Dodging the facts hinders real learning. Your performance, whatever it was, was the best it could have been at the time. Accept it. Physical strength, your technical skill, your ability to focus your mind, your level of motivation, and many other factors all contribute to performance. Saying, "I could have made it if only I had really gone for it," is similar to saying, "I could have made it if I was a better climber." Knowing how to commit to the climbing, jamming a difficult crack, being comfortable on small footholds—these are all skills which take training to refine, just as building strength does. You're facing the facts more clearly when you say, "I think that moment of hesitation shut down my commitment." Instead of wasting attention on regret or "could have" thinking, accept full responsibility for your performance, analyze and learn from your experience, and lay the groundwork for a stronger effort next time.

The goal when assessing the climber is to see the skills and abilities as they are, without blowing them out of proportion, being overwhelmed by the lack of them, or allowing them to predetermine how you'll perform. Different types of climbs will require different types of skills and abilities. For example, sport climbs at Rifle Mountain Park in Colorado will require endurance and face-climbing techniques, whereas trad climbs at Devils Tower in Wyoming will require endurance and crack-climbing skills. Find out what skills will be required and assess them objectively. For now, we simply want to clearly observe the skills and abilities that will impact our performance. Later, in the Giving process, we'll focus on how to utilize those skills to create the best performance.

The last step of assessing is fully accepting what you've found. Don't lapse into wishing you'd found larger holds, more pro, safer falls, or stronger arms. Accept what you've found so you can collect the necessary information in order to see the situation as clearly as possible.

We began this chapter by noting some common obstacles to objectivity: association, metaphor, and memory. Then, we detailed a simple objective risk assessment, noting several places where our objectivity might be suspect, and devoted some attention to the element of falling. Last, we noted how the Ego might come back after the fact and cloud the assessment we made while in the risk situation. Let's now elaborate in more general terms on the art of honesty and accepting responsibility.

Radical Honesty

You cannot act effectively upon a lie. If you are not honest with yourself, your attention will be wrapped up and weakened by deception. The facts you might use to deal with challenges won't be reliable. We lie to ourselves as a way of shirking responsibility for acts or outcomes that make our Egos uncomfortable. We do this in several ways.

Earlier, we mentioned wishing, hoping, and victim thinking, typical mindsets that keep us from accepting a situation as it is and taking responsibility for dealing with it. Now let's examine specific ways we shirk responsibility: blaming, denial, excuses, pretending, and justifying.

By *blaming*, you transfer responsibility to someone or something, thereby absolving yourself from acting to change the outcome. For example, during a redpoint effort you pull for slack to clip a bolt, but the belayer doesn't give slack quickly enough. In the process of clipping the rope, you fall. You blame the belayer.

You can choose to hold your belayer responsible for the outcome, but how much does that help? What was your part in the belayer holding the rope too tight? Did you instruct him on how to belay you? Perhaps you even noticed he was keeping the rope a bit too tight. You wanted the rope tight because you were fearful, and then you hoped it would pull freely when you needed it. Maybe you even saw the problem coming but knew you were pumping out and wanted the excuse of getting tight-roped on the clip. Even if you instructed the belayer to keep the rope loose, and he was totally responsible for holding it too tight, what is the best way to respond? Will you focus your attention on blaming the belayer, or save that power to do something to improve the situation?

Denial is another way to shirk responsibility and lose power. For example, you go for a redpoint effort and don't redpoint. Then you say, "I was just practicing." This is denial behavior. You're not being honest about your intention. You say you were practicing when, in fact, you were having trouble fully going for it. You're ready to redpoint, but you're stalling. Why? You don't know, and denial isn't helping you find out. In fact, you have a motivation issue, which is no different than a strength issue or a technique issue. Denial is keeping you from approaching your motivation issue with the same straightforward problem-solving tactics you'd apply to figuring out a sequence of moves. Don't indulge in denial behavior, which only creates illusions and reduces your ability to see how to improve.

Excuses behavior also causes us to shirk responsibility. You may say, "My forearms are too weak." That may be partly true, but what else contributed to your arms getting pumped so quickly? What about your breathing, your balance, how you paced yourself, how much you were overgripping, or how much pro you placed? It is very common to use the excuse of weak forearms as a reason for falling. There are many, many reasons, however, why your forearms might have become so tired in the first place. Inherent weakness is probably not the most significant one. Regardless, that excuse simply diverts attention from applying skills to conserve forearm strength and climb the route.

You might *pretend* that climbing well isn't important to you. If you state, "I don't care about climbing well," you're probably pretending. You pretend in order to dull the disappointment of a substandard performance. You're coddling your Ego. You aren't being truthful. Pretending that climbing well isn't important makes it more difficult to climb well.

Like pretending, *justifying* behavior is a way of coddling the Ego: "I couldn't do it, but no one else could do any better if they were in my shape." The Ego is running the show here using its typical ploy of comparing your performance to others—as if that had anything to do with learning or personal power. You've justified your external performance while conveniently sidestepping the real issues, such as why you are out of shape, how well you climbed given your level of fitness, and what you could learn from the experience as a whole. You focused your attention on justifying your performance instead of learning from it and figuring out how to improve. What a waste of power!

These behaviors not only drain attention away from the effort, but they direct that attention into negative work. They creates illusions, making it more difficult or even impossible to analyze what really happened in the experience and to learn from it.

Face Reality

The action word for the third warrior process is **Accept**. This word will remind you of what Accepting Responsibility encompasses: clearly grasping the reality of a challenging situation by collecting objective information and dealing with that information honestly. This accepting process will help us understand the ways we often delude ourselves and choose a passive role instead of taking charge of our destiny. By accepting responsibility for as many factors as possible we maximize our field of influence and minimize the power lost to factors beyond our control. By accepting things as they are and discovering exactly how they are, we gain power. We stop wishing holds were better, stop hoping to miraculously make it up a climb, stop blaming poor performances on weak forearms, inattentive belayers, or global warming. We accept responsibility in order to claim power.

As we accept these responsibilities, we grow to accept a great truth: life is difficult. Once we fully accept difficulty as natural and normal, we cease to be offended or daunted when we encounter a struggle or a test. We can embrace these tests as opportunities. Difficult experiences are the way we learn, and they also are the way we can appreciate ease. We understand brightness by its contrast to dimness, happiness by its relationship to sadness. By embracing this duality of experience, we allow ourselves to find peace within our difficulties rather than wasting our power on trying to escape them. We shift to a position of power by focusing on seeds of opportunity within difficulty and staying curious, by exploring reality instead of avoiding it.

Chapter 4
Giving

The Accepting Responsibility process examined reality. We discussed being honest about our role in events in order to claim power, and how to recognize traps set by the Ego tempting us to shirk responsibility. We discussed the art of gathering objective information in order to dispel phantom fear. The warrior process of Giving uses discovered facts, and the acceptance of them, to actively create a powerful attitude for entering the challenge. The Giving process helps us focus on what we have to *give* to the effort rather than on the difficulty of the challenge. Giving is our last preparation step before beginning the transition into action.

Our society encourages an achievement orientation, but is less effective at encouraging the effort that leads to achievement. We love "get-rich-quick" schemes. We play the lottery. We indulge in dieting schemes that promise we will lose weight while sleeping or by simply drinking a chocolate shake. Perhaps human beings are inherently lazy, but these pervasive influences in our society conjure up a false reality in which results can be achieved with no effort on our part. Many of us grow up believing we are "owed a living," that it is society's obligation to offer us a satisfying way to make a living rather than our own responsibility to invent one.

In general, we are socialized to have a *receiving* mindset. Driven toward the imaginary American Dream, we are not encouraged to be appreciative and grateful for what we do have. We're conditioned to think we will be happy when we obtain: that new car, that promotion, our lottery check. The same mentality appears in our climbing. We think we will really enjoy climbing when we get something: stronger forearms, more free time, the redpoint on our project.

With a receiving mindset we slip into thinking we have a *right* to be happy, and we are somehow *entitled* to what will make us happy. We may work diligently, but in our minds we are waiting—waiting to receive what we think we deserve. The real world doesn't work that way. We don't have a right to be happy. Nor will any specific outcome automatically make us happy. What we do possess, that no one gave us or can take away, is an ability to learn and grow. Taking advantage of this ability, however, always requires real effort. We have to give something. The more we give, the more we will receive—regardless of the specific outcome. It is the combination of giving and learning that brings happiness. This is the essence of the warrior Giving process.

The Giving mindset is rooted in an attitude of being grateful for what we already have. We can't manifest the giving spirit if we feel slighted. If we have not currently attained our goals, that is fine. We should not, however, interpret that to mean we have received less than our "entitlement." The warrior rejects the very concept of entitlement. Entitlement thinking is passive. It sets us up to wait. If we feel we are entitled, we are less inclined to make a strenuous effort to achieve an outcome. Entitlement thinking also implies that we have more wisdom than we actually do. Do we really know what outcome would be most beneficial in the long run? Would we ever learn anything if we always received the outcome we thought we deserved? Personally, when I think about what I've learned in life, I am grateful not only for the comfort, but the setbacks and challenges that have made me who I am.

Even though we've been discussing philosophy at length, the Rock Warrior's Way is not about building up an edifice of abstract ideas. It is about developing a practical frame of mind that works for improving performance. The essential point I'm making is that if we lapse into a receiving mentality, as might be our habit in life, then performance suffers. We become passive and separated from the real situation. We focus on things we don't have or that don't even exist. The traps may be obvious when we consider the lure of shiny cars, diet drinks, or lottery tickets. However, the mentality spills over into our climbing and affects the way we think about the strength in our arms, the holds we use, or the gear we'd like to place.

Things we don't have can't help us solve the challenge before us. Thoughts of unlimited forearm strength, bigger holds, or an extra protection bolt can only cloud reality, drain away attention, and make our progress more difficult. Instead of regretting what we don't have, we can focus our attention on feeling grateful for what we do have. This makes us feel empowered. If we are glad to have this tiny edge on which to place a toe, glad for that cam ten feet below us, glad, even, that the rock in front of us is demanding rather than easy, then we feel rich. Feeling rich, we are ready to give—to give our best. This frame of mind wields power.

Expectation

It's important to go into a climbing challenge with confidence. Overconfidence, however, shows a misunderstanding of, and disrespect for, the challenge. You are involved in a subtle dance with expectations. With rigid expectations about how you will perform, you don't leave room for the process to unfold or for learning to take place. With no expectations, you may not hold yourself to the highest standard. It's too tempting to take the easy way out if the climbing becomes uncomfortably strenuous. The key is to place your expectations not on a specific outcome, but on an attitude of possibility, effort, and learning.

Expect that it is possible to do a climb, not that you will. When you expect to get up a climb, you're engaged in a form of entitlement thinking. It is one thing to feel you are capable of doing a climb—that's helpful. It's another thing entirely to assume your ability guarantees a certain outcome. The moment you have the thought, "I expect to make it up this climb," you project yourself into the future when the effort is over. This drains attention from the effort itself, reducing your effectiveness. Your effort is what's important. It is your act of giving. Without giving, learning or growth is not possible. The exercise becomes rote and motivation drops. As you enter a climbing challenge, make sure you expect to make an effort.

If you give yourself fully to the challenge, you can expect to learn something. Embrace that expectation. A learning expectation keeps motivation high because you will receive what you want from each step of the process, regardless of how hard the route is or how far you make it. With an expectation of learning you're focused on gathering new information. Your attention stays focused in the moment, increasing your effectiveness.

Routes near your limit offer the greatest opportunity for learning, but they become recipes for frustration if you have a results-based expectation. You expect to be able to climb them, having climbed this level before, yet this expectation drains critical attention. Since routes at your limit require all of your attention, skill, decisiveness, and com-

Expect to be challenged, and to learn. Facing the great unknown on Quartz Mountain, Oklahoma. Photo: Shullphoto

mitment, anything less than 100-percent attention will likely cause a fall and frustration when your expectation is not met. Frustration quickly saps your motivation, since you're not getting what you want. When motivation drops so does commitment. Without commitment, you lose the ability to produce a maximum effort. You enter a downward performance spiral.

Frustration is a sign that your attention has faltered. You sought out a challenging objective, but you're forgetting why. Instead of diving into the rich learning process such a climb offers, you want the challenge to come down to your level. You're disgusted, and you want it given to you. "I should be able to climb this route," you say. That's entitlement thinking. You're not even thinking about how to sharpen your skills to the level the climb requires, which was the whole point in the first place. Your attention has drifted toward receiving and is further tied up in "poor me" behavior. You want something for nothing!

If you find yourself becoming frustrated, take it as a symptom that you are out of alignment with your goals. If you really want an easy success, find an easier climb. If you want a real challenge, you've found it. If the Ego is asking for a trophy to use in its externally oriented game of self-worth, look the Ego dragon in the eye and draw your sword. Then pay attention, give your best, and enjoy the ride.

FOCUS

The action word for the Giving process is **Focus**. In Accepting Responsibility, you used your full attention to develop a clear, detailed, and objective idea of the situation. Now your goal is to focus attention onto engaging the situation, onto the challenging task at hand. Mentally, you will move toward the situation.

In the Accepting Responsibility process we objectively assessed the three parts of the situation: the route, the fall consequence, and the climber. Doing this gave us tangible and accurate information. When we assessed the climber we identified certain skills and abilities that would impact the performance. Our previous level of mastery in those skills is an objective quality, not so different from hold size or rock angle. Our application of those skills in a new situation, however, is purely subjective, and that is our focus in Giving. In the Accepting Responsibility process we assessed our abilities so we could get an idea of the "toolbox" from which we could draw to engage the new challenge, and not let ourselves become overwhelmed by phantom fears about the apparent difficulties. Now, in the Giving process, we'll focus on how to utilize those tools, our existing skills and abilities, to create the very best performance. If we focus our attention and give our all to the effort, even if we don't make it up our route we'll expand our comfort zone and increase our skills. That's the goal. The Giving process, however, can be sabotaged if we fall into a receiving mindset.

Receiving

By saying, "I want to get this redpoint," you aren't focusing on the impending challenge. You're adopting a receiving mindset that separates you from the task at hand and diverts attention from the quality of your effort. Put aside thoughts of the outcome and focus on the grand effort about to take place. Honor it. By asking, "What can I give to this effort?" you position yourself for engaging the challenge.

Focusing well is an art. Many of us have a tendency to focus on what we don't have—skills we don't possess. Wayne Dyer, who has written many books on self-actualization, calls this tendency *deficiency motivation*. It's the old water-glass concept. You think your glass is half empty, forgetting it's also half full.

With deficiency motivation, you create a mental image of repairing a "bad" situation. Think of a skill like thin-hands crack climbing. A deficiency-motivated person says, "I don't know how to squeeze my hand to get it to hold in thin cracks." Rather than falling into deficiency motivation, you can focus on actively improving the existing situation. Think of building upon skills you already have. For example, "I do know how to squeeze my hand to jam in hand-size cracks. Let me modify that process for thinner cracks." You automatically start thinking how you use your thumb against your palm, press with your fingers, etc. You've framed the task in such a way that you have something tangible to work with and build upon.

Other examples of deficiency thinking include focusing on the unknown ("I can't see what's up there"), or on impossibilities ("I can't do this move"). Let me describe an experience I had a few years ago where shifting my focus from impossibility to possibility made all the difference. It was on a climb called *Steepopolis* at a sandstone cliff called the Tennessee Wall near Chattanooga, Tennessee. *Steepopolis* is a trad route, rated 5.12a, a bit runout, and takes thin wires and small TCUs for protection. It's not a straightforward climb because it doesn't have the typical, obvious T-Wall horizontal handholds. I climbed up about forty feet to where the crux began, continued into the crux, and fell.

The piece I had below the crux was bomber, so I wasn't in danger. The crux wasn't obvious, however, and the next protection placements were difficult to see. I looked up and said to myself, "I don't see where I can get any pro," and, "I don't see how to climb this crux." I gave a few half-hearted efforts, but each time I ended up hanging on the piece below the crux. I was stuck for thirty minutes in my passive, impossibility mindset.

Finally I woke up and realized what I was doing. I said, "Arno, you teach this stuff. How about focusing on possibilities?" I looked up and said, "If there is a possibility for pro, where would it be?" I saw a small seam

which looked like I could possibly get something in it. Then I asked, "What sequence could work, if anything could work to climb this crux?" I noticed some side pulls, so I decided these could possibly work to climb through the crux. I began working with the side pulls and climbed to the seam. I found a rest, placed a small wired chock, and continued up the route.

My initial focus had been on what I didn't see and what I couldn't do. As soon as I shifted to a position of power where I focused on possibilities, I was able to climb the section that had stumped me. When I was stalled out, I had been talking to myself in statements. After I made the power shift, I began talking to myself in questions. These questions helped me to retrieve my attention from being tied up in passivity and use it actively to figure out what I could see and what I could do. After that, the doing fell quickly into place.

In Accepting Responsibility, you focused on objectively describing the route's holds and the climber's skills. In Giving, you use this objective knowledge to create a plan of action. There is something about the route that will challenge you. Identify it and focus on what skills you'll use to rise to the challenge. Those skills include ones you have now and the improvements you might make on them, as well as new skills. Rising to the challenge also includes maintaining a possibility mindset, which creates possible solutions to the challenge. You don't see a foothold that's "too slanted to stand on." You see a foothold that could work well with a sidepull handhold.

This possibility-focused thinking, applied to your effort and abilities, creates the giving attitude. You can't give what you don't have. You can't give your lack of perfect jamming technique. You can only give the technique you have, plus your effort to improve. Giving helps you tap into the familiar skills and abilities you typically climb with, and new possibilities you discover.

Room to Believe

The Giving mindset is focused on the how, the process: how to protect, how to jam, how to pace yourself. It isn't about climbing cracks smoothly. It's about learning to climb cracks smoothly. It's not about being powerful. It's about learning to become powerful. If you keep your focus on giving effort and learning, then you'll continue to improve skills like climbing cracks, placing pro, and becoming powerful. These skills aren't end results. They are in a constant process of improving.

The author on steep terrain at the Tennessee Wall. *Photo: Jeff Achey*

Remember, the warrior's goal is power. Simply having the skills doesn't increase personal power. Power increases through the process of enriching those skills, which you do by throwing yourself into situations where you dip into the treasure chest of the unknown.

Radical Thinking

A sport like climbing progresses through possibility thinkers. Generally, standards are inched up by adding small developments to what already has been achieved. We stand on the shoulders of what others have shown to be possible. Once in a while, however, a John Gill or Reinhold Messner appears who radically changes our concept of what is possible.

In the 1960s, John Gill did boulder problems that were far beyond the normal difficulty of the day. Soon after he began climbing, Gill found that his inclinations differed from those of the mainstream climbers around him. He wasn't interested in Himalayan peaks or Yosemite walls and didn't feel they had any connection to what he enjoyed, which was climbing very difficult moves on small rocks. Gill took an activity that was considered practice, a mere sideshow to real roped climbing, applied his full focus to it, and declared it a worthy activity in itself.

Reinhold Messner brought an entirely new outlook to climbing the world's highest mountains. Himalayan climbing had become a complex exercise in logistics and tactics with ascents often requiring months. Messner, however, preferred the freedom of the climbing style used in his native Alps. To make the first "alpine-style" climb of an 8000-meter peak, Messner simply applied enough confidence and fitness to make his preferred climbing style work on a much larger scale. Messner quickly decided many mainstream climbing perceptions were not supported by satisfactory evidence. When Messner and his partner Peter Habeler announced their goal of climbing Everest without bottled oxygen, the "experts" declared the feat impossible, saying oxygen deprivation would cause severe brain damage. The pair demonstrated otherwise. Now, many mountaineers have climbed Everest without bottled oxygen.

Gill and Messner raised world standards, but the important lesson is not how their feats compared to others. Their advancements came through radical, creative thinking, casting off the shackles of what they were being told. Each of us has such shackles which can be cast off. When we think in new ways, we foster creativity. What our old selves called impossible, our new selves may claim can be done. We see new options, potentials, and possibilities. Just as nothing standard-setting can be done with a mentality of "that's the way it's always been done," so will we be held back by clinging to the mentality of "that's the way I've always done it." We may never set world bouldering standards or sprint up Himalayan giants, but we can experience our own revelations of what is possible if we are willing to think radically.

Impossibility thinking is based on rigid opinions, and it's focused on negative abilities. Possibility thinking is based on options and it's focused on positive abilities. It's important to see possibility within yourself, to believe you have the potential to meet big challenges. Your habits form imaginary walls, but outside these walls, there is room to believe. It's easy to fall into impossibility thinking. Since it shrinks the world, such thinking can make us feel secure. Security should be our base camp, however, not the field in which we play out the adventure of our lives. Observe yourself, be alert for stale thinking, keep focusing on learning, and you'll surprise yourself by what is possible.

Think in possibilities, not just little possibilities but big ones. Give yourself room to believe. You're more capable today than you were last year and will be more capable next year than you are today. Believe in that future potential. Be radical. A warrior is a leader, not a follower. Remember, however, it's each person's responsibility to take the appropriate amount of risk. Each individual must find that fine line between life and death, no-injury and injury. This will be a continual process. You push yourself further and further into possibilities and the unknown, and return with more personal power to risk again another day.

Chapter 5
Choices

In all endeavors there is a moment of truth. Preparation time is over but the action has not yet begun. The gun goes off for the sprint; the curtain comes up for the dance performance; the person you've been collecting the nerve to call picks up the phone and says, "Hello?" Your mindset in the following seconds has a huge impact on the course of events.

Climbing is full of these moments, and the climber is particularly active in orchestrating them. A skier or kayaker is almost thrown into his challenges by the force of gravity, but the climber is offered a more extended period of choice. Climbing gives us more opportunity to either rush or procrastinate. Unlike a paddler in a surging river, the climber on a rock face can step up ... and then step back down. The static medium of rock places full responsibility on us for timing our choices and following through. We can waste vast amounts of power through tentative, ambivalent, incomplete choice-making or by second-guessing a well-made and well-timed choice.

The Risk of the Comfort Zone

People, climbers included, naturally tend to seek security and comfort. Within the familiar context of our "dangerous" and "adventurous" sport, we still resist extending ourselves into insecure and uncomfortable situations. We have trouble leaving that large handhold or that bombproof cam, even though no learning is taking place there. It's important to reaffirm our commitment to learning and remind ourselves that we really do want to make "risky" choices.

Paradoxically, taking risks actually increases our safety and comfort. Sudden danger lurks everywhere—losing our jobs, being struck by a car, contracting a mortal illness. A cowering, protective approach to life doesn't reduce the peril. It only serves to make us slaves to fear and victims of constant anxiety.

The safety, comfort, and security we crave aren't objective states. They are subjective feelings that come through increasing our understanding of our world and our capabilities. In short, we gain comfort and security by expanding our comfort zones, and we expand our comfort zones by venturing into the risk zone. We make ourselves uncomfortable and insecure for a short time in order to learn what we're capable of. We can't directly attain comfort and security; we must strive for them indirectly.

The Right Choice?

Choices are not right or wrong, good or bad. Life would be a bit boring if it was so simple. You never know the full, long-term ramifications of a choice. Conscious choices are more like tests of our knowledge, providing opportunities for concrete lessons on the ever-wandering path of knowledge.

Let's say you've been climbing for a couple of years, and you're now moderately proficient at arranging protection and understanding protection systems. How did you get to that state? Were you making "bad" choices as a beginner when you chose five different nuts before finding one that best fit the crack? No, you were simply learning about how nuts work in a very effective way—experimentation. That's an easy example of "bad" or "wrong" choices being simply part of the learning process. Let's look at a less obvious example, a choice we'd be more likely to call "bad," one with serious consequences. Suppose you're a more advanced climber and you know how to quickly place solid gear. You're at your local crag, pushing yourself on a short route, and you decide it's safe to risk a fall on a crux move. You blow the move, fall, and swing unexpectedly into an obstacle, badly spraining your ankle. You're taken totally by surprise. The obstacle was well out to the side of your gear and nowhere near where you were climbing. Your climbing day is over. Two other climbing parties are involved in your rescue. Worst of all, it will be weeks until you can climb again, by which time you will have lost that fitness edge you worked so hard to gain.

You certainly aren't rejoicing in your choice to go for that move ... but was it a "bad" choice? You learned a lesson about fall dynamics in a way you will remember. A year later, you find yourself in a similar situation facing what you once considered a safe fall. This time you're 2000 feet up on a remote climb in Alaska. Because of your "bad" choice a year earlier, you realize that a swinging fall here could slam you into a nearby dihedral. You rearrange the protection to create a longer, scarier, but safer, straight-down fall. Despite a strong effort you fall off and land unhurt. You go up again, make it through the section, and continue on the climb. Your "bad" choice a year earlier very likely just saved you from taking a dangerous, swinging fall and involving you and your partner in an epic, multi-day self-rescue.

A small mistake one day prevented a big mistake on another day. "Bad" choices often teach you something and become more valuable than the "good" choices. The warrior knows this and foregoes the "good" and "bad" designations altogether. A warrior is involved in the process of discovery, in the great adventure, and what he seeks is knowledge. Good and bad are misleading concepts, which imply we know more than we actually do. There are many lessons to learn, and we're never sure ahead of time exactly what lesson we're learning. The warrior wants to preserve his life and continue on the journey, but he also knows he must take risks in order to explore life.

If "right" and "wrong," "good" and "bad," can't guide us, how can we choose? If falling off and spraining an ankle might be "better" in the long run than avoiding that fall, shouldn't we just throw ourselves into experience and hope for the best? If we can't know beforehand, why should we bother putting so much thought and energy into assessing risk and making conscious choices?

If you go to Italy but don't understand any Italian, you won't learn as much about Italian life and culture as you would if you spoke the language. The same applies with risks and yourself. If you don't understand the components of the risk you're facing, your learning will be commensurately limited. Avoiding "good" and "bad" doesn't mean you should adopt an attitude of total relativism or ambivalence. The problem, rather, is that those particular words have baggage. They are constructions of the Ego. We tend to use those words based on whether an event made or will make us comfortable. The Ego is impatient. We're too likely to attach "good" and "bad" to the immediate impact of events. We forget that "good" may set us on a collision course with misfortune and that "bad" may be a saving grace. By judging events in such a black-and-white manner, we dishonor and dismiss the subtleties and richness of experience.

There is, however, a guidance system for the warrior in lieu of good/bad, right/wrong. The warrior calls it the *heart*. To follow *the path with heart* is to follow a kind of very personal "good," one that is more

Commitment in a nutshell: giving it all on a small-holds dyno. *Photo: Shullphoto*

open, humble, and attentive to the deeper workings of the universe where we ultimately draw our strength and energy. "Good" and "bad" appear to us when we're responding to Ego-based, external motivation. The path with heart appears to us when we are infused with a love-based, internal motivation. Loving what you do, being in touch with what you truly value, will help you make choices in any area. A path with heart is essential when making choices about risk. A possibly dangerous choice should

not be made carelessly. It must be aligned with a person's innermost predilections, stripped of the dangerous and superficial trappings of the Ego and self-delusion. Love-based motivation creates a situation without regret. When you make a choice, you choose to live life the way you most want to live it. Only when you're functioning in such a mode can you summon the near-magical power of 100-percent commitment.

Investigating Falling

Falling, perhaps because of its dynamic and counterintuitive nature, seems to be a stronghold of phantom fear and deserves some extra focus in our discussion of choice-making.

Our goal is to create a clear set of choices that will yield simple, yes/no answers about what we are willing to risk. Most climbers will decide that some falls are safe enough to take, while others are too risky. In Choices, our focus is on putting our money where our mouth is, fully accepting a fall that we say we're willing to accept.

In practice, such acceptance is no easy feat for some climbers. People who begin climbing in a gym and on sport climbs often become accustomed to taking lead falls. They learned how to fall safely when they were still relative beginners. People who learn to climb on traditional crags, however, are generally more conservative about taking lead falls. They first needed to learn how to place solid gear, and they also climbed on lower-angled terrain where falls are more dangerous. The habit of resisting falling tends to linger, even when you know how to place solid gear and climb on steeper rock. Fear of falling is very common, even among sport climbers, and it is not caused by simple fear of injury. Falling involves a feeling of losing control. One moment, you are firmly attached to the rock, doing everything possible to maintain that attachment, and the next moment you are free-falling through the air.

When no significant danger exists, fear of falling is another manifestation of phantom fear. The Choices process addresses totally accepting the possible outcomes of your effort. One possible outcome is that you will fall. You don't want to simply push this possibility out of your mind, since this will create an unconscious attention leak, perhaps a large one. You want to fully accept the falling outcome.

One example of fear of falling, and how to manage it, took place on the first free ascent of the *Salathé Wall* on El Capitan in 1988. This was the

Falls—such as this one at Hueco Tanks, Texas—are part of climbing, and the best way to develop your aerial skills is to practice. *Photo: Beth Wald*

hardest, longest, free climb yet done in the world, and the climbers were very skilled and experienced. On the Headwall pitches, over 2000 feet off the ground and fiercely exposed, Todd Skinner and Paul Piana were truly challenged. The difficulty of the climbing was so close to their limit that any bit of lost attention was enough to shut them down. They bivouacked on the wall for days while working on the Headwall cracks. During this time they

---

HAVE A SAFE FLIGHT

Falling is an important tool for the climber, but I do not mean to imply that it isn't dangerous. Even a short fall can hurt you. Falling involves an unavoid-able loss of control where many factors come into play. If your belayer is inattentive or inept, he can drop you or cause you to slam into an obstacle. If you haven't been paying attention to your rope sys-tem, your rope may run over a sharp edge that could cut it in a fall.

When assessing the fall consequence, consider not just the distance from protection, but also how the climbing lines up with the pro, the angle of the rock, and the position of the pro relative to over-hangs. If you are to the side of your protection you will swing during your fall, possibly hitting an obstacle unexpectedly in your path. Jumping in the direction of your last pro will reduce the swing and the possi-bility of hitting obstacles. If the route is overhanging, some extra slack in your belay rope may help you avoid hitting the rock as you swing inward. If your protection is placed under a roof that you then climb over, you have created a situation where a fall will tend to slap you back against the wall below. In this case the belayer can feed slack to lessen the impact against the wall. For detailed falling practice see the Exercises.

---

noticed they were distracted by fear of falling, especially first thing in the morning. That's not hard to imagine, considering their position. To deal with this leak of attention they began each day by purposely taking progressive-ly longer falls: fifteen feet, twenty-five feet, and finally forty feet. After this practice session the jitters were gone. They fully accepted the fall conse-quence and could focus all their attention forward into the climbing process.

How do you accept a fall? Realize that falling is a natural part of the climbing process. Modern ropes and gear provide great freedom to push your limits in climbing without taking undue risk. To take advantage of this freedom you need to become familiar with falling. If you haven't fallen regularly then you will tend to resist it. Also, falling safely takes some practice. You can hurt yourself even on very short falls if you wrap the rope around your leg, hit a small ledge, or swing sideways into an obstacle. You need to learn how to respond to these hazards if you want to fall safely. I suggest making falling a part of your warm-up each time you climb. This way you embrace it, develop some proficiency at it, and see it as a tool and a skill you can comfortably apply to solve a climbing challenge. If you don't develop this proficiency and familiarity, you will leak attention into fear of falling and have less to focus forward into climbing.

Commit to What?

Deciding to take a risk—what does this mean? What, exactly, is the form of your decision? It is crucial to choose an appropriate goal to commit to and to know exactly what that goal is. Otherwise, you may define your choice too rigidly, eliminating useful options, or too vaguely, opening yourself up to fear and second-guessing.

Climbing involves constant testing and exploring. In earlier chapters we discussed in detail how to gather information on a route. In this chapter we're focusing on the process of moving into action. You've sketched out the risk you're going to take, and now you want to take it in the most powerful way possible. On a runout trad climb, that risk may be a very small part of the total climbing challenge, perhaps only a single move up to a hold or possible gear placement. To climb through a single runout, you might make several separate risk decisions. Even a sport redpoint will often break down into smaller risk events and decision points. For each decision point, however, no matter what type of climb, there are only two possible outcomes: you climb through the risk or you fall. In order to take the risk most effectively you must absolutely accept either outcome. If you can't do that you need to redefine the risk or back off.

After exploring and experimenting, decide upon a specific opening sequence for the first moves that separate you from the unknown. That's your initial focus, just those moves, and you'll go for them 100-percent. Beyond those few moves, your information is incomplete. Your plan must be more flexible, but you don't want to confuse flexibility with vagueness. Your plan needs to be as clear as possible so you will be able to commit 100-percent. Above your opening gambit you may have in mind several specific possibilities you've worked out in advance, or you may simply decide to see what holds appear and climb the moves on intuition. Your mindset is flexible yet firm; you will climb through to the end of the risk or fall off in the process of that effort. The end of the risk may be the top of a climb, the next bolt, or a point you've worked out in advance where you can reassess the climbing possibilities and falling consequences. The key is to decide ahead of time, eliminating the temptation to second-guess. This mindset will send you into the unknown with an optimized combination of intuition, decisiveness, physical effort, and mental relaxation in an open and full-hearted engagement of the difficulties.

A risk need not involve physical danger. The mind can feel threatened by many different things, potential bodily injury being only one of them. When facing a difficult redpoint, you engage a different kind of risk, and the unknown you're setting off into is of a more abstract type. You know exactly what you want to do physically—the moves, the rests, etc. So why are you feeling anxious? The key to completing the climb may not be figuring out a hard move or mastering the fear of a scary fall. It may be finding that elusive combination of will, strength, precision, motivation, and relaxation that must come together to see you to the anchors. The way you begin the climb, and your commitment mindset, play a large role in determining how easily you're able to keep the conscious mind from leaking attention into distractions, such as your desire to make the redpoint or anxiety about blowing a low-percentage crux move.

The best performances involve maximum, efficient effort with the body and no effort with the conscious mind—a state of relaxed concentration. Your conscious mind should feel satisfied that it has prepared you for the risk. Feeling confident of what is ahead, the conscious mind can back off and allow intuitive processes to take over. This allows information to flow easily from your subconscious into the performance. We'll talk more about how to stay "in the flow" during the risk in later chapters. For now, let's return to the moment of truth.

Entering the Risk Zone

Andrew Jackson said it well: "Take time to deliberate, but when the time for action arrives, stop thinking and go in." Preparation is over. It's time to be decisive.

We often hesitate to fully face a risk, and this is quite apparent as we approach those moments of truth. Instead of embracing the excitement of the moment, we often engage in inept ploys to blot it out. Some climbers have a habit of edging into a risk without consciously committing to it, and suddenly find themselves in over their heads. This is their trick for pushing themselves to do something they're too fearful to do with full awareness. They then have to "sink or swim," and in essence, have avoided the choice-making act altogether. Another trick is to rush into a risk before the reality has had time to register. Doing this avoids the anxiety produced by the decision-making process instead of confronting it directly.

Neither of these approaches is an effective strategy for creative risk-taking. Attention is distracted, minimizing the empowering aspects of the experience while maximizing the actual danger. In contrast, the warrior's choice-making involves impeccable use of attention.

The Choices process is about directing your full attention in a specific direction, either into the risk or toward a definitive escape from the risk. Remember, *not taking the risk* is an essential option. Choosing not to take certain risks is part of the path to knowledge and power. Simply assessing a risk and working toward preparing for it are valuable learning activities. The Rock Warrior's Way is definitely not a method for pushing yourself into foolish risks. It is a method for cutting through the mental clutter, gathering your attention, discerning exactly what the risk is, deciding if the risk is appropriate for you, and then fully committing your resources to your choice. You decide the appropriateness of a risk by comparing the new situation to situations you've already faced. You weigh the fall consequences against your experience with responding to such consequences. Everything—the moves, the reserve strength you have left, the fall consequences, your level of motivation—is on the table. With this clarity you make your choice.

The Rock Warrior preparation processes—Becoming Conscious, Life is Subtle, Accepting Responsibility, and Giving—lay a sound foundation for marshalling mental resources and assessing a risk. If we've prepared well we have as much information as possible about what we're facing. The preparation processes also collect and focus attention, making it powerful enough to punch through our natural resistance barrier that defines the edge of our comfort zone. Now, should we choose to take the risk, our task is to direct our full attention into it. We've collected all the power available. More power can only be gained by stepping off into the unknown.

Unbending intent

Directing attention into a choice involves more than simply shifting focus. It should be a dramatic, cathartic event. Attention focused in the direction of a choice is a new entity: **intention**. A warrior's intention is a powerful force. He intends to do something, intends to take action—not casually but with all his being. Don Juan called the moment of decision the warrior's *gate of intention*, and the mental state of a warrior, once he passes through this gate, one of *unbending intent*.

Unbending intent means 100-percent commitment into the risk zone, total engagement of the challenge presented by the route. There may be flexibility in the specific choice of moves, as intuition dictates, but the will to move forward is fierce and unbending. The Choices process is the art of decisiveness. The word decisive derives from the Latin *decidere*, literally, "to cut off." You cut off what's no longer necessary: the unchosen options, the uncertainty and dispute. You cut off all possibility of hesitating, doubting, and wondering. The immediate future becomes very simple. You commit completely to a single course of action.

Total commitment is more than just saying you'll do something and then doing it. Powerful things transpire when you fully commit. W. H. Murray can help us realize more of what is happening in this process with his passage on commitment in the book *Scottish Himalayan Expedition,* which ends with a couplet from Wolfgang von Göethe:

"Until one is committed there is hesitancy, the chance to draw back, always ineffectiveness. Concerning all acts of initiative (and creation), there is one elementary truth, the ignorance of which kills countless ideas and splendid plans: that the moment one definitely commits oneself, then Providence moves too. All sorts of things occur to help one that would never otherwise have occurred. A whole stream of events issues from the decision, raising in one's favor all manner of unforeseen incidents and meetings and material assistance, which no man could have dreamt would have come his way. *Whatever you can do, or dream you can, begin it. Boldness has genius, power, and magic in it.*"

As you keep your attention 100-percent directed into the risk, you'll obtain assistance from unseen forces to help carry you through the risk. What unseen forces? The unseen forces are the unlimited potential of your subconscious. Have you ever surprised yourself while climbing? Climbed something you didn't think you could? Most climbers have experienced this. That surprise happens when the conscious mind is transcended and the subconscious is allowed to manifest some of its unseen forces.

The Bullet and the Laser Beam

We can visually represent our life and actions with two graphics that I call the Bullet and the Laser Beam. They give visual structure to our concepts of the comfort and risk zones and provide a model for understanding the warrior processes.

There are several components of the Bullet. The entire diagram (plus the area beyond the paper) represents your potential. The area inside the inner circle represents the part of your potential that is your present comfort zone: what you know, the realm of your ordinary world, what is comfortable. Everything within this circle is potential you have already realized. An example might be your ability to lead 5.10 sport climbs. You've experienced many 5.10 sport climbs and are comfortable climbing them. You aren't scared, but rather can focus on and enjoy the climbing experience.

The ring-like area between the inner and outer circles is the risk zone. What lies in the risk zone is unknown to you. This zone is a teacher—you might also think of it as the learning zone. It represents experiences you haven't gone through, or experiences that make you uncomfortable. Everything in the risk zone is potential you haven't yet realized. Let's say you are comfortable on 5.10 sport climbs but have little experience on trad climbs. On 5.9 or 5.10 trad climbs you will have a tendency to be scared, have difficulty focusing, or have difficulty enjoying the climbing experience because there are aspects of trad climbing you haven't experienced, such as placing pro. These experiences are in your risk zone.

Figure 5.1: The Bullet

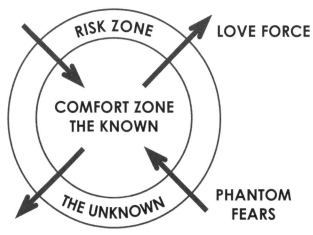

The inner circle that defines the risk zone represents the resistance barrier between the comfort zone and the risk zone. You feel this barrier during a challenging experience. You feel resistance to leaving the comfort zone and venturing into the risk zone. The outer circle of the risk zone represents the outer edge of a particular risk. Beyond this lies realms of the unknown that are not accessible during the particular risk you're modeling.

The final components of the Bullet are the "force arrows," those originating inside the comfort zone and going out into the risk zone and the others going in the opposite direction. There is a force pushing you out of your comfort zone. You can call this force desire, but I call it the love force. It is your desire to engage life, to take on challenges, to take risks. The love force creates situations where you learn more about yourself.

The inward-pointing arrows represent the force that keeps you in your comfort zone. This force derives from fear. I call it the phantom-fears force. This force restrains you and keeps you inside your comfort zone. It makes you resist the unknown. This force isn't "bad." It is quite necessary, because without it you would be soloing 5.13s and killing yourself. To take appropriate risks, however, you need to weaken this force so you can expand your comfort zone. You weaken the force by eliminating or reducing phantom fears. You accomplish this by focusing attention on the love force rather than the phantom-fears force.

By engaging a risk you seek to expand the inner circle—your comfort zone—toward the outer circle. After having taken the risk, you will have expanded your comfort zone to include some of what was previously part of the unknown.

The Laser Beam

The Laser Beam adds the seven Rock Warrior processes to the Bullet graphic. A laser collects light and concentrates it into a beam that has more power than unfocused, disorganized, ordinary light. The warrior "laser" collects and concentrates *attention*. When you focus your attention like a warrior, you concentrate it like a laser beam concentrates light, producing an intention with concentrated power analagous to a laser.

The preparation phase takes place in your comfort zone: attention is collected, centered, directed, and focused so that it can become powerful enough to punch through the resistance barrier of the inner circle. Punching through the inner circle is the graphic representation of the transition phase, the Choices process. Your attention is now like a focused

Figure 5.2: The Laser Beam

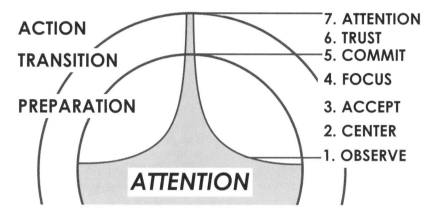

laser beam, bursting through the inner circle into the adventure of the unknown. The last two warrior processes, subjects of Chapters 6 and 7, keep the "attention beam" from dispersing (losing its focus) during the action phase of the risk.

Love and Commitment

We touched earlier on an important key to decisiveness and commitment: motivation. When a challenge is large, you need to be in touch with heartfelt motivating forces in order to embrace the task at hand.

In 1978 I was traveling around the West on a climbing trip with my brother Mark. I had an experience that shows how love-based motivation can energize you and help you commit. The commitment was of a slightly different type than we've discussed in previous examples. It was the more drawn out kind of commitment you need to head up onto a big wall, but the role played by motivation is the same as on a shorter climb.

We had climbed many classic routes on the trip and our last goal was to climb the Diamond on Longs Peak in Colorado. We had climbed for a while in the Boulder area and, feeling confident, we decided to go up to Longs. We packed everything we needed with the intention of camping below the wall, climbing the face in one day, and walking out on our third day. We chose to do *D7*, one of the shortest and easiest lines on the wall, in a mixed aid/free fashion. During our walk up, we felt confident and excited about climbing such a great alpine face—until we saw it. The face was huge, much bigger than anything we'd done before. The desolate alpine cirque, beautiful as it was, made the wall even more intimidating.

The Diamond and the east face of Longs Peak, Colorado. *Photo: Jeff Achey*

After a few minutes of imagining ourselves on the wall, with plenty of negative self-talk going on, we escaped back to Boulder. We decided we would climb in Eldorado Canyon for the rest of our trip.

After the first day of climbing in Eldorado our thoughts drifted back to the Diamond. The beauty of the face and the fact that we had chickened out without giving it a true effort spurred us to go back. The next day we hiked up and camped below the wall. The face was just as intimidating, but we passed the afternoon by scoping out the approach, the route, and the walk-off. We decided to get up early the next day so we'd have plenty of time to climb, but woke up at 6 AM—not exactly an alpine start. Despite our late start we decided to go for it, although we both had in our minds that we might not fully commit. By 9 AM we were on Broadway, the large ledge below the Diamond proper.

On Broadway I felt suddenly fueled by what I love about climbing: the setting, the exposure, a steep wall, and a degree of unknown. The alpine beauty of the place, which had been daunting, was now inspiring. We looked down on our camp and felt we had already embarked on a great adventure, even though we could still easily escape without facing the actual Diamond. Thus inspired, we began climbing and completed pitch after pitch without incident. We arrived at the top after nine hours on the wall, having made a great leap into the unknown and come out on the other side.

By identifying with our fear of the unknown we had shut down the possibility of climbing the Diamond. We had allowed ourselves to be overwhelmed. Without coming to grips with the route, how could we know if we were capable of climbing such a wall? Yet how could we come to grips with the route if we didn't believe we were capable? All big challenges have this element of ambiguity. By tapping into what we loved about climbing we were fueled to engage the route and let the experience show us if we could do it or not.

The key factor was that desire to engage. We didn't know whether or not we could climb the wall. We *did* know that we could engage it. When you engage the risk, you focus your attention on the process, not on the outcome. You focus on moving up, but you keep the channels open. You set an intention you can believe in: to engage the risk. Don't set an intention of "making it up the climb," since you don't know for sure if you can. Instead, accept the two possible outcomes—making it up or not making it up—and focus on joining with the risk. Blending the new information coming from the risk with what you observed in the preparation phase and what you bring from your previous experience creates new learning. In the case of the Diamond, the new information was that being up in a wild, exposed place that previously intimidated us was energizing. The exposed position was an unexpected source of power, just the extra power we needed to climb the great wall that had been our goal.

The Moment of Truth—a Snapshot

So far in this chapter we've examined the preparation side of the "gate." We discussed how the sport of climbing has decision points that are particularly poignant, and how comfort and safety are paradoxical terms. We discussed how to find a foundation for choice-making in a very unpredictable world. We discussed the two possible outcomes and the need to become familiar with falling. We analyzed intention and the kind of commitment needed when facing a risk. Now we'll turn to the dynamics of the crucial moment and the beginning of powerful action.

You often hear of the fight-or-flight response to moments of danger or risk. This is not part of the Rock Warrior's Way. If you assess a risk and choose not to take it, you do not flee. You disengage, consciously and in control, without panic. If you choose to take the risk, you do not fight. You engage and embrace. I sometimes hear climbers say, "Fear energizes me to climb. It motivates me and helps me climb." These statements betray a shallow power base. They show, first of all, that the climber lacked motivation. The climber overcomes his low motivation by creating fear. He falls into a destination-oriented mindset to escape the fear, fighting toward the end of the climb. Lethargy, fear, and a struggle to "get it over with" are not aligned with the true warrior goal: learning. Physiologically, the fight-or-flight response is accompanied by surges of adrenaline, which lead to the use of excessive force and quick consumption of energy. These are not characteristics of efficient climbing.

If you're using fear to motivate and energize you, you're showing a symptom of a more significant problem which is probably affecting your entire ability to enjoy climbing and improve: being out of touch with your love of climbing. Instead of jarring yourself with fear, tap into your love. On the Diamond, I found that the remote wall put me in touch with deep motivation, enabling me to overcome my aversion to discomfort and the unknown. Finding your true motivators can help you overcome obstacles between you and your inner desire to learn and explore.

You're almost ready. Now, form your unbending intention. The action word for the Choices process is **Commit**. Create a clear distinction between the time of weighing your options and the decisive moment of choice, between preparation and action. The transition must be abrupt and definitive. Create a moment of truth, a sharp breaking point. Every fiber in your being must know that you aren't preparing anymore; you are going into action.

Until now your conscious mind has been involved in extensive internal dialogue, assessing, exploring, and gaining focus. You have accumulated all the intellectual knowledge possible about the unknown realm you want to experience. You accept the two outcomes, making it or falling. Don't go before you are ready, but when you go—go! Now you set out in quest of experiential knowledge.

As you make the break, the conscious mind will shut down all its chatter. Subconscious and intuitive processes take over. Once you begin moving, the conscious mind becomes a silent and observant passenger carried along on the wings of power.

Chapter 6
Listening

When you commit to action you are in a place of opportunity and exhilaration. The calculations are over. You are fully living the moment and fully giving of yourself. The difficult climbing facing you is not an obstacle or an emergency, but rather an intense learning event. Your goal is to participate openly in the challenge and not become distracted by a desire to control the creative chaos of the situation. Our natural aversion to discomfort will tend to call up "comfort thoughts" from the conscious mind. These thoughts lure our attention away from the challenge to an imagined comfort zone at the end of the effort or into wishing and other escape behavior. It's important to dispell these thoughts and stay in a receptive state, blending new information with what you already know.

When you're in action the body takes over from the conscious mind as the key actor. You're acting out the risk, not thinking about it. Like a dancer, you stop thinking and simply move. When you pause, or a sense of discomfort overtakes your involvement in movement, the conscious mind will attempt to reassert itself. Your goal is to minimize this interference. Since your goal is to not think—even about *not thinking*—you'll quiet the conscious mind through body-oriented methods: continuous breathing, continuous climbing, and soft-eyes focus. You can reflect on this process as you read about it here, but during the action your focus will be to disengage the conscious mind from thinking.

You have committed to action with unbending intent, yet climbing allows many chances to hesitate and rethink. You're in the process of smoothly on-sighting a difficult sport climb and you reach a big handhold. Suddenly you want to cling to the sense of control you have at your stance. You linger on your island of comfort and a brief, helpful rest drags out into hesitation. You find yourself trying to control the situation rather than trusting in the process. Your intent begins to bend.

Experimenting with moves and planning out a sequence gives you control over a climbing situation. That's helpful. Allowing controlling behavior to take over when it's not contributing to knowledge is not helpful. I experienced this in 1978 while climbing *Hollywood and Vine* on Devils Tower, Wyoming. The route follows a thin 5.10 crack on the southeast face. The grade of the climb was very challenging for me at the time. News that a climber named Henry Barber had recently soloed the route seemed to interfere with my ability to open up to the route. Maybe I was vaguely imagining myself up there unroped as Henry had been, and I was half afraid of falling to the ground. Maybe I felt inept because I was finding the climbing difficult while someone else had been so comfortable he didn't even need a rope. In any case, I was holding on harder than necessary as I climbed to where the crack thinned to a seam. I continued up a few feet on delicate face moves but felt out of balance and tense. I didn't want to go for it without knowing what holds were there, even though the fall was safe. I made a half-hearted effort on the next move and fell.

Even though I hadn't given a strong effort, I told myself that I wasn't

able to do the climb. The fall relaxed me a bit and I liked the feeling of being supported by the rope and equipment, so I began aiding the crack. As I aided up I saw some edges—which I would have discovered had I made a strong effort the first time—and realized I could do the moves. I decided to go back down. Next time up I climbed the thin seam section free without taking another fall.

First time up I was intent on controlling the situation instead of trusting in the process. I was resisting falling, overgripping, and hesitating. These behaviors held me back from giving myself fully to the effort and paying attention to the possibilities of the route. The second time up, with some new information, I trusted in the process. By falling once I accepted the fall that had bothered me earlier. By relaxing my grip, staying in balance, and climbing continuously, I stayed receptive throughout the process and made it through.

Why couldn't I simply have trusted in the process the first time? Somehow I developed a weak and distracted frame of mind early on the climb. Climbing through a challenging section of rock can resemble conversation. In conversation many people stop listening to what's being said. Their attention becomes focused on why they agree or disagree with some early remark. They plan ahead to what they'll say next, even though their remark will probably be out of context at that time. They end up channeling their energy into defending their old set of beliefs instead of being open to the possibility of learning something new from the speaker.

The same thing can happen in climbing. Suppose you happen to climb a section inefficiently, such as I did on the lower part of *Hollywood and Vine*. You tend to hold on to the sensation of that action. You expand it into more climbing inefficiency by dragging it from the past into the present, compromising your attention on the task at hand and eroding your confidence. Or, you might encounter a troublesome move and decide that a higher move, too, will give you trouble. Instead of facing the challenge openly and optimistically, you form an expectation of trouble.

You may not realize it, but these distractions are heads of the insidious Ego dragon. We immediately recognize the Ego's role in our conversation example: the person is preoccupied with his own ideas and isn't listening to others. He is self-centered and out of tune with the flow of conversation. He tries to control the conversation because his agenda is set by the Ego, which doesn't care about new ideas or learning. It's looking for approval, and it wants to show either the superiority of its own habitual ideas, or the ability to dictate the conversation. It's the same in climbing when you

Devils Tower, Wyoming. *Photo: Jeff Achey*

become rigid. You're preoccupied with preconceived notions and with your actions. You're defensive rather than curious. You want a sense of control, even if the only way to attain it is by clinging to a mediocre level of performance. You're looking for an escape from the discomfort of the effort and you aren't Listening.

If you find yourself clinging to a large hold or to the sensation of an inefficient move, remember that this is part of the Ego's agenda. Draw your sword and slice off the dragon's head. By slaying the Ego you become free to stay receptive and to listen to what's happening in the moment. By listening, you suspend your limiting perceptions and old beliefs. Habitual perceptions and beliefs will take you to your previous levels of performance—and no further. If you want to exceed your old boundaries you need to create a new and expanded understanding. Not only must you enter the risk zone on the rock, you must enter it in your mind. Just as you leave the comfortable stance and launch out onto steep, smooth, unknown stone, so must you let go of those comfortable notions that define what you think you can do. The risk zone is the learning zone. As Albert Einstein said, "No problem is solved with the same level of consciousness that created it." The Ego won't bring you to a new level. You must listen to the unknown.

Listening

"Listening" is a metaphor for the mindset you're striving for as you climb. Listening is not something you do just with your ears, but rather is an entire way of staying receptive. When you're too focused on a rigid, specific plan in your climbing you'll tend to squint your eyes and create a sense of concentration in your forehead and temples. When you open up a bit and adopt an attitude of receptivity, your face relaxes, creating a soft-eyes focus, the role of your eyes becomes less overpowering, and the focus of sensation moves back toward your ears. Receptivity is the basic attitude of listening, which is very different from seeing. We can see only in the direction we look, but we can hear from all directions at the same time. When we listen, we're paying attention to our whole environment.

We tend to overlook or not recognize an unexpected discovery when we're narrowly focused. Being too selective compromises our receptivity and therefore our learning. For example, while climbing into a crux,

Henry Barber, master soloist of the 1970s, ropeless on the sea cliffs of Gogarth, North Wales. *Photo: Edgar Boyles*

you move over a roof by pulling on edges. As you move up you find the wall above also has a hidden finger crack. An unreceptive climber will tend to dismiss this unexpected discovery and stick with his original plan of face climbing and looking for edges to grab. A receptive, "listening" climber will use the unexpected crack as a clue to modify his approach from face climbing to crack techniques.

Specific expectations in general are antagonistic to a listening mindset. In the Choices process we talked about setting an intention and introduced the concept of unbending intent. Unbending intent might seem opposed to a mindset of listening, but it's not. The beginning of your action may involve predetermined moves you are certain of, but after those moves, your intention must be able to accommodate new information. Your intention isn't to put one hand here and one foot there. It's to continue climbing through the risk or to fall. In other words, you make a 100-percent commitment to effort and action, not to some specific set of techniques or moves.

With your intention set on the outcome you tend to map out your course in advance and develop rigid expectations about the moves you'll do. These expectations ruin your ability to climb spontaneously. When the situation changes, you must revise your plan. It takes precious time to withdraw your original plan and redirect your intention to a new plan. Your new plan, of course, involves new expectations. As you continue climbing into the unknown and the situation changes again, you repeat the process. This constant withdrawing and reapplying of intention makes your climbing choppy and rigid, rather than fluid and spontaneous. Being unattached to any specific expectation, in contrast, places you in a receptive state that allows you to pay attention and listen to the rock. Your intention stays in the moment. When the situation changes, you don't need to waste time redirecting your intention. You remain focused through the entire effort.

Dihedral climbing is an appropriate example of the importance of listening. You set off up the dihedral with the rigid intention of laybacking. You climb the dihedral for a while but the crack becomes too small for your fingers. You continue laybacking on fingertip holds until your original approach becomes so inefficient and strenuous that you're forced to stop. Just before you pump out and fall you reconsider your plan. You look around, see holds on the face, and begin stemming. Pleased with yourself, you stem up, but soon you're climbing with the same rigid mindset as before. You continue stemming but suddenly notice that for over a body length now, the crack has been wide enough for hand jams. So, better late than never, you switch to jamming. A bit higher, the crack pinches down with you still in jamming mode. You make an all-out effort to jam strenuously through a thin-hands section and barely make it to easier climbing.

Figure 6.1: Listening Climbing

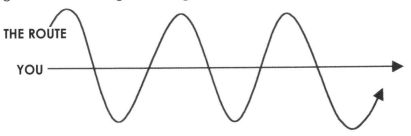

ABOVE: Rigid climbing technique on a climb with varied demands.
BELOW: Varied technique flowing spontaneously on a varied climb.

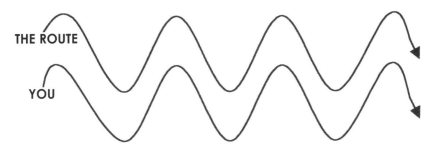

Obviously, this ascent involves a lot of wasted energy. You set rigid expectations concerning what you would do on each section of the dihedral. Initially, if you had set one expectation—to learn and trust yourself—then you would have created a receptive frame of mind that would allow you to climb spontaneously with a natural mix of techniques. Your continuing question would have been, "What does this dihedral offer to allow me to climb it?" You would have stemmed earlier and avoided the strenuous fingertip layback moves, moved smoothly into hand jamming as soon as the crack opened up, and laybacked easily through the thin-hands section where you almost fell.

An open expectation can also apply to your sense of difficulty. If you expect a climb to feel difficult, you may become locked into that feeling. You may overlook options because you've already decided that a maximum effort will be required. Remind yourself to remain open to holds or techniques that might conflict with your preconceived notion of difficulty.

You can open up your attitude concerning difficulty itself because difficulty is a state of mind. What feels difficult for one climber might feel easy for another. This perception often has more to do with attitude than

physical strength. As you begin climbing into a crux, your intent should not be only to move upward but to loosen your rigid perception of the "difficulties." The word difficult is derived from a negation of the French word *facile*, meaning easy. It's a negative construction—"not easy"—with a negative emphasis. It's comparable to saying "not ugly" to mean beautiful. Rather than seeing a crux as a "difficult" place lacking easy passage, see it as a challenging place offering the opportunity for learning. This more open mindset can be very powerful and help you enter enthusiastically into the effort. A sense of embracing opportunities and opening up to possibilities is an important tool for transcending perceived barriers.

Within your unbending intent to climb into the challenge, you'll keep an open, attentive mind. Remember, your level of receptivity determines your speed of learning. If the conscious mind begins to engage in thinking, direct your attention to your breath, which helps put the conscious mind in neutral. See and feel the holds and moves as they are, without perceiving them as good or bad, easy or hard.

Intuition

In modern culture, intuition is a vague and often derided faculty. The analytical, left-brain part of the mind tends to ignore or negate intuitive knowledge. To the warrior, however, intuition is specific and crucial. It is his connection to hidden information and unrealized potential. If you block the intuitive flow, you block out very important information.

Intuition is not logical. We can't analyze how or why we intuitively know something, yet most of us have had experiences that convince us intuition is real. Don't confuse true intuition with inner dialogue. Intuition comes from your subconscious and tends to manifest as very clear and specific feelings about doing something. Inner dialogue manifests itself as more ambiguous and thought-intensive messages, typically related to the concerns of the Ego.

Recently I returned home from a Sunday climbing outing and had an encounter with intuition. I was putting my climbing gear in the garage and had the apparently random thought to put the child seat in the truck. I keep the child seat for my son, Ian, in the garage with my climbing gear. Immediately, my left-brain logic dismissed the thought. I shouldn't need the child seat until Tuesday, when I take Ian to daycare. I didn't put the seat in the truck, but I noticed this mental transaction between my intuition and logic and told myself I would pay attention and see if there was a need for

Dihedrals offer many options for climbing. Avoid tunnel vision! *Photo: Shullphoto*

the seat. As soon as I walked into the house, my wife, Jane, asked me if I'd pick up Mexican takeout. Ian immediately asked if he could come along. I put the child seat in the truck and went with Ian for the Mexican takeout.

Somehow I received non-logical, intuitive information about the unfolding situation at my house after climbing. There are various ways to attempt to explain this rather mysterious phenomenon. Developing situations, such as my wife's desire for Mexican food, may manifest some sort of energy that is silently communicated to the subconscious mind. It is not important or possible for us to completely explain intuition. It is important to realize that it works when given the chance. Intuition, being outside our logical framework of ideas, is free from the agendas and preconceived definitions that limit us. Intuition is a precious point of access to the unknown, which is the ultimate source of all new knowledge and power.

Develop your receptivity to intuition. When you receive an apparently random thought, don't simply discard it. Stay curious and follow it. See where it leads. Intuition whispers to you between your conscious thoughts. Listen to those subtle thoughts and feelings just below the level of your consciousness.

The following methods will help you improve receptivity to intuition while climbing:

• Observe yourself. By separating and observing yourself from the Witness position you will recognize intuitive messages more readily.

• Breathe continuously. Breathing continuously helps dissipate anxiety and also keeps you in the moment. When you're in the moment, intuitive information can flow more easily.

• Be open and curious. If you're closed and clinging to fixed beliefs, you don't allow information to flow into your awareness. In *The Gift of Fear*, Gavin de Becker tells us that "curiosity is the way you answer when intuition whispers."

• Find your center of gravity and keep it in balance. The average person's center of gravity is about one inch below the navel. Keep that center in line with the arm you're hanging from, the foot you're standing on, or poised equally between your various points of contact. When you are out of balance, your attention is distracted by the need to deal with that unbalanced state. When your center of gravity is balanced, attention is available to notice subtle intuitive messages.

• Be nonjudgmental. A judgmental attitude ignores or discredits intuitive information, making it difficult to recognize. Gavin de Becker suggests that a dog's keen sense of intuition is partly due to its inability to judge. You can produce a nonjudgmental state by focusing on options and possibilities instead of opinions and evaluations.

• If you speak to yourself, speak in questions. When you ask a question, in a sense, you send a demand to your subconscious to supply an answer. It answers through your intuition.

• Finally, follow your eyes. Intuition operates through your eyes to direct your movements. In *The Power of Silence*, don Juan states that intent is summoned with the eyes, and in *The Fire from Within*, he relates that your eyes are the keys to entering into the unknown. Your body naturally wants to be in balance. Your intuition, through your eyes, will direct your movements to find a balanced position. Your body has knowledge. Pay attention to how your eyes direct your movements and trust them. (The level of balance and efficiency of this direction may depend on your level of climbing knowledge and experience.)

Deepak Chopra, the author of many books on understanding your essence and contacting your spiritual self, calls intuition "heightened awareness." It is always truth. You never have false intuitions. Falseness can only occur during interpretation of intuitive messages, as you relate to them from a perspective of phantom fear, wishing, or limited beliefs.

We often think of normal perception as being very objective compared to intuition. It's not. We don't simply see or hear, passively and objectively. Rather, perception is the complex mental act of organizing sensory information through the lens of past experience. We hear a loud bang and we hear a gunshot, a car backfiring, or a screen door slamming. Which one we hear depends not so much on the sound as on our mindset and our context. In other words, we *create* a large portion of the perception. Three different climbers see a certain rock feature and variously perceive: a strenuous layback crack, a delicate stemming problem, a dangerous, unbolted trad route. These three perceptions are tainted by past difficulties, fears, expectations, and beliefs. All are limiting. The reality of the rock contains a far greater range of possibilities.

The point is that our perception can't be completely trusted, yet we must rely on it for information. The warrior seeks a heightened form of perception. He disciplines his mind so that his ordinary perceptions are more in line with a love of life and thirst for learning, and less inhibited or tainted by past experiences and fear.

To access the truth and its possibilities we need to stop tainting it with preconceived notions and phantom fears that hold us prisoner in our comfort zones. The world is what it is. The truth is out there and accessible through an open-minded approach and intuition. We need to develop our intuition so that its whispers are familiar and frequent.

Being in Control vs. Being Controlling

In climbing, being out of control can be dangerous. It's not a desired state for general climbing. There is a difference, however, between being in control and being controlling. Being in control is the state where you work efficiently and process yourself through the risk. You show mastery over your mind and body. Being controlling means that you try to control things that can't be controlled. You try to create comfort in the risk zone by clinging excessively to the elements of security within the risk.

Be aware of controlling aspects when you climb through a risk. Signs of being controlling include climbing slowly, climbing too statically, resisting or dreading falling even when it's safe to fall, overgripping, holding your breath, grabbing pro, down climbing excessively, and placing more pro than needed. These behaviors waste energy and attention and reel you back into the comfort zone when you need to be moving forward into the climbing process. The Preparation and Choices processes allow you to create a situation where you can fully give yourself to the risk. Rather than clinging and backpedaling, enjoy the freedom your warrior preparation allows.

Trust

You move up a smooth, committing face to a possible protection crack. Upon arriving you find the crack is less useful than it looked from below. Don't fight the facts. Go with them. Relish each new revelation. This is your incomplete, intellectual knowledge of the risk being corrected through experience. You are now in the process of achieving your highest goal—learning. Accept the situation as it is. Trust the process.

Trust bridges the gap between your ability to assess the risk beforehand and your ability to rise to the actual challenge the risk presents. Keep a possibility mindset. Stay with your intent. Don't, however, confuse possibility with hopefulness. You aren't *hoping* for any specific outcome. Your goal is learning, and that's being achieved. Simply trust in the process. You'll climb through or fall, and either outcome will provide learning.

When you are in the chaos of the risk zone, the conscious mind often will revolt. It is outside of its realm, the comfort zone, and if engaged in the thinking process, the conscious mind will create thoughts of comfort. When you are in the risk zone, your conscious mind will generate various thoughts to convince you that you can't continue climbing. These thoughts are pure deception. The conscious mind is a liar when it is engaged in thinking while in the risk zone. A trusting mindset keeps the conscious mind disengaged from thinking.

Observe your thoughts from the Witness position. Don't be drawn in by them. When comfort thoughts arise, let the thoughts go and stay with your intention. You'll accomplish this not by arguing or reasoning with the conscious mind, which takes you even further off task, but rather by doing something with your body. Breathe, consciously and continuously. Shifting your focus from the intruding thoughts to your breathing makes a bridge back to the body, to the flow of action and movement. Keep moving. Don't wait for perfection. Use the holds you grab. Listen to Saint Nike: "Just do it." Climbing continuously makes it difficult for the conscious mind to keep up, to reassess the situation, or create fear. Continuous climbing creates momentum that overwhelms thoughts. The conscious mind gives up and disengages from trying to control the action. By disengaging the conscious mind and positioning it as the passive observer, you allow intuitive information to flow from your subconscious into your climbing experience.

In my old home area of Fremont Canyon I had two experiences that exemplified the conscious mind sabotaging my climbing efforts. In the early 1980s I was working on a new route called *Sword of Damocles*. The route is 300 feet long with the crux on the third pitch, a six-foot roof split by a thin-hand crack. The wall above the roof opened up to hand size and then wider. After several efforts, my partner, Steve Petro, led the pitch free. Then it was my turn to climb. I gave several efforts that resulted in falling. Each time I'd go back down to rest and give it another go. The thin crack in the roof was very strenuous and the crack above was a little too wide for solid hand jams.

Each time I gained the crack above the roof, I'd think I was too pumped to trust my jams and would fall. Instead of staying focused and giving my best effort, I would rebel against the discomfort and insecurity of the climbing. My conscious mind stepped in and told me I could not do the moves. While I was sitting on the ledge between efforts, I couldn't think of any alternate way to do the moves. When I reached the insecure section I'd stall out, struggle, and give up.

Steve was becoming pretty bored by now at the belay, and I was becoming exhausted. On my last effort, I decided I would do whatever was necessary to make it work. I was as pumped as ever as I began climbing the crack above the roof as I'd done earlier, with widely cupped, straight-in hand jams. The insecure jams began to slip out, but I kept climbing. Intuitively, I leaned my body into a position where I was laybacking slightly off the jams. My hands still felt insecure in the wide jams but the change of position was enough to keep them from slipping out of the crack. That was enough to keep me from falling and I finished the pitch free. Once I shut off the "quitting" thoughts generated by my conscious mind, continuous climbing and intuition provided a way to climb the crux.

Not long after *Sword of Damocles*, I was working on a short crack climb called *Superman*. My brother, Mark, and I had worked on freeing it several times and continually were shut down at a section of overhanging crack with wide finger jams. At the time I had little experience on this size crack, and each time I got to the crux, the jams felt too tenuous. My conscious mind, confronted with this unknown type of jam, was sure my fingers wouldn't hold. In essence, my conscious mind lied to me by telling me the jams weren't secure enough to pull up on. In fact, my conscious mind did not know whether the jams were secure enough or not. All it knew was pulling on those jams was outside its comfort zone.

On the day I redpointed the route, I climbed up to the crux and, for no apparent reason, pulled on the tenuous finger jams and was able to make a move up, then another, and another. After three or four moves, I was through the crux and continued to the top.

I didn't know the mechanics of why the jams held, but they did. I gained new knowledge of what kind of jam could hold and used this knowledge on many later climbs. I only gained this knowledge, however, by continuing to climb when my conscious mind told me I couldn't.

Once you commit, your mindset becomes one of action. You disengage the conscious mind. You allow the free blending of information you've gained in the preparation phase with new information you gain as you climb. Let intuition guide your exploration of the unknown, because your conscious mind cannot.

Trusting the process on an overhang at the Shawangunks, New York.
Photo: Jeff Achey

Remember, your highest goal is learning, and only in action does true, experiential learning occur. This is what you climb for. In order to transcend a risk, you need to learn something, and you'll only be able to learn by staying open and receptive. In your preparation for the risk, you've meticulously set specific parameters to avoid serious injury and safeguard your life. You've decided that the risk is appropriate and that you want to take it. Your art now is to participate in the risk in the most empowering way possible. You've committed. Disengage the conscious mind and trust in the process. Remind yourself of this with the action word for the Listening process: **Trust.**

Chapter 7
The Journey

The preparation phase of the Rock Warrior's Way focuses on understanding how our conscious minds work. We play little tricks on ourselves that drain power and inhibit our performance. Fears, real and imagined, can negatively influence our behavior under stress. Recognizing fear and the various kinds of fear-based motivation allows us to develop a more love-based foundation for action. Love-based motivation moves us from an avoidance orientation toward a learning and seeking orientation, which focuses our attention more sharply on the task at hand. The whole process of meeting risks and challenges becomes not only more efficient, but more enjoyable and rewarding. This increases our motivation and willingness to put ourselves in challenging situations. Thus, the Rock Warrior's Way places us in a positive feedback loop, a path that continuously increases the personal power we have available when entering into risks and challenges.

In the transition phase we focused on creating a 100-percent commitment to action. The preparation phase helped us to do this, since through it we have a much better idea of exactly what the risk is. We've examined the risk scrupulously, made plans that limit the danger, and resolved questions about our intent in risking. We also developed specific psychological strategies for fully committing to the process.

Now, in the action phase, we keep ourselves mentally in the action, in the most empowering frame of mind possible, despite our natural tendency to seek escape. The Listening process concentrated on opening up the subconscious and intuitive information systems and limiting the role of the conscious mind. The final process, the Journey, focuses on keeping attention in the moment to find comfort and meaning in the risk.

When we are in the chaos of a risk, our attention has a tendency to seek an escape. It wants to leap ahead to a place of comfort, such as the top of the climb, the next protection, or the next rest. We need to learn to keep our attention focused in the present chaos, where it can work for us.

The Rat Race

Early in our lives we are taught to be competitive and value achievement and results. We are encouraged to "make something of ourselves" or to "get ahead." The emphasis is on a future destination, for which we will sacrifice the satisfaction of the present. Ironically, once we arrive at a destination—landing that sought-after job, climbing that 5.12 grade—we find it's not a final destination at all. We aren't satisfied to stay there. We may even look back nostalgically to the passion we possessed when we considered that destination a magical promised land, before we realized it was simply the end of a journey. Inevitably we begin a new journey, and a new one after that. In fact, our entire lives are spent journeying.

The warrior is the ultimate realist. He knows that life is a journey, and rather than rushing blindly toward the next destination, he appreciates the journey itself and consciously lives within it.

The destination mentality is the way of life in normal society, and we tend to adopt it by default in situations of acute stress and discomfort. When we come to an uncomfortable climbing situation, a strenuous offwidth crack climb for example, we immediately look up to determine where the effort will end. Seeing only ten feet until we can rest, we may feel energized, completely capable of moving up. If we see fifty feet of effort, however, we're demoralized and can't summon the will to move up that same ten feet. That ten feet of climbing is the same in the second situation, but *we* are different. Our attention has moved out of the challenge and into the future. If we could remain focused on climbing—the journey—then we wouldn't sabotage our effort with anxiety about the distance to a destination. Often, that ten feet of effort will lead to new knowledge that we won't discover if we give in to discomfort.

Discomfort is one stimulus for destination thinking, and chaos is another. We are socialized to avoid chaos. Schools condition us to work in a highly structured environment and break down learning into tasks to be performed in an organized way, one by one. The ability to organize is an important skill, but sometimes an experience can't be organized and broken down. Committing to a crux section of unknown rock is an example. We must take it as a whole and deal with it.

How often have you said, "Once I get this problem figured out, then I can really get down to business?" Here, you're postponing what you want to accomplish until you can create a serene, ideal environment. Typically, that perfection never materializes. The chaos continues, and it paralyzes you. Why not simply get down to business, chaos or not?

In a risk situation in climbing, you constantly enter the unknown. So much new information comes in that it's impossible to complete one task before beginning another. Most of us don't have skills to deal well with such chaos. When our normal, step-by-step mode doesn't work, we tend to panic or rebel. When we encounter chaos, we try to get rid of it rather than go with it. The warrior knows that's not possible, and seeks to find internal harmony in the midst of chaos.

Purposely seeking out risks allows us to practice dealing with chaos, but often our reaction is to mentally "leave the scene." We passively wish for the chaos to simplify and resolve itself. In fact, when we stay relaxed and stop wishing and hoping behavior, we maximize our effectiveness to function amid chaos. The key is to accept the chaotic nature of the experience and give it our full attention. We accomplish this acceptance with a journey mindset.

The destination mindset is also responsible for "failure" and "success" anxieties. Success and failure are in quotation marks here because a warrior doesn't use these terms. He doesn't see the result of his effort as success or failure. Making it up a climb may be his provisional goal, but the higher goal is learning. The warrior does not know what end result will yield more learning.

Perhaps, you dread "failing" on climbs, specifically the repeated "failure" when redpointing at your limit. You desperately want to avoid the anger you feel when you fall, the guilt you feel for your lack of commitment or training, or regrets you harbor about eating too much the night before. These feelings drain the joy from your efforts. You reach the point where all you want is to finish the climb so you can stop those feelings of failure.

Alternately, you may experience success anxiety. This mindset isn't negative like failure anxiety, but it still distracts precious attention away from the moment. When you get past a crux and "success" is in sight, you become protective of your effort up to that point, as if somehow it could be lost. You become detached from the process and attached to the reward you expect if you finish the whole climb. "Don't blow it," you say to yourself.

At this point, you're no longer interested in the act of climbing; you just want to have climbed the route. You get to the crux, or past the crux,

and anxiety sets in, a fear of losing the success you've imagined is near-ly yours. Obviously your attention is not working to your advantage here. You are focused negatively on not losing an ascent you have not yet even finished.

In both success and failure anxiety, you lose focus. By over-valuing the outcome and under-valuing the process, you focus on the destination. Once you do this, climbing is pointless. You close yourself off to the pres-ent moment and you do not learn. You simply want your body to catch up with your mind, which is already in the comfort zone at the top of the climb or back on the ground basking in glory.

One of the most obvious symptoms of destination thinking is nervous-ness before and during a redpoint effort. You're very motivated to *have done* the climb, and the thought of the effort and uncertainty separating you from your goal stresses you out. Some climbers also experience a strange loss of motivation once they've worked out the moves on a climb and made a few redpoint efforts. This too is caused by the destination men-tality. The climb is "as good as done." You "know" you can do it. Yet the real challenge and gut-level learning still waits. With a "good as done" attitude, the actual performance becomes an obligation rather than a chance to enter the risk zone and hunt for power. Thus, motivation wanes.

Success and failure do not exist in the present, only effort and action exist. You reach for a hold, step out over an overhang, surge up into a hand jam, and fall free through the air. These exist in the present. Success and failure are later constructions, phantoms created by the Ego. The Ego has no use for learning and it does not like chaos. It wants a trophy list of destinations with which to validate itself. The Ego will try to escape from the chaos of the risk zone to a comfortable destination even though it sab-otages your effort by doing so.

Paul Piana, an expert climber with many first ascents to his credit, related a story that shows the power of a journey mindset. In 1996 he had been working on redpointing a project climb, *Atomic Cow*, at Wild Iris, a sport-climbing area near his home in Lander, Wyoming. One day at the crag an out-of-town friend showed up. "I told him about a really nice 5.13 that I had been working on that had really nice moves on it," Paul told me. "I hadn't been able to redpoint it but wanted to show him the moves. I got on it without any expectations other than to show him how sweet the moves were." To Paul's great surprise, he floated through the moves and made the redpoint. With his focus on the great moves rather than the red-

It's a long ride, so enjoy it. Savoring every foot of *Rock Lobster*, Indian Creek, Utah. Photo: Jeff Achey

point, he found just the "relaxed concentration" he needed to maximize his performance. By not thinking of his destination, he reached it.

A student of mine, Jeff Jenkins, had a similar experience while climbing in the Obed River area of northeastern Tennessee. He had been working on a well-known 5.12 called *Tierrany*, a very steep route that climbs out multiple tiered roofs. He had made several redpoint efforts over several days and returned on the last day before he and his partner were moving on to another climbing area. "I had pretty much accepted the fact that *Tierrany* wasn't going to go that day," related Jeff, "but I wanted to take one more lap just to see whether I had finally figured out

the crux." Jeff had accepted that the redpoint could wait for another trip and had become more interested in simply testing his knowledge of the route. As a consequence, his attention was completely on the climbing rather than on success or failure. He went up the route in a very relaxed, curious frame of mind. "Lo and behold, next thing I knew I was through the crux and shaking out before pushing to the anchors!" exclaimed Jeff. A minute later he finished the redpoint, one of his most satisfying to date.

Destination thinking causes a disjointed mindset that hinders performance. The physical body always operates in the present, but the conscious, thinking mind always dwells in the past or the future. You cannot have a thought about the present moment; in the time it takes to form the thought, the moment is already gone. When you are in the risk you need direct, immediate perception, not the lagging commentary of the conscious mind thinking about what is happening. When the conscious mind is engaged in thinking, a gap is created between your body and your mind. Fear enters through that gap, and attention leaks out.

In the Journey mindset, in contrast, there is no room for fear. Failure does not exist in the present, nor does the intellectual baggage that comes with it. Success, too, is irrelevant. The Journey mindset rests on learning and expanding personal power and doesn't rely on the subordinate goal of making it up a specific climb. You may really want to do a certain climb. That's natural. The Rock Warrior's Way, however, teaches that too much attachment to such goals isn't effective in achieving them. Learning and personal power are the actual goals. If our efforts are firmly directed toward those deeper goals, then we're able to reach our climbing goals more effectively.

The Journey mindset is love-based and ready to engage the risk. It's not rooted in escape or avoidance as destination thinking is. When you love the challenge, you freely give your attention to it. You are in tune with the flow of the experience. You aren't fighting it, avoiding it, or wanting to end it.

Journey thinking also increases your post-climb rewards. If your attention isn't in the present during the experience, you won't remember the experience very well. The details are vague. You can't remember the texture of the rock or the sensation of suddenly intuiting elusive moves and flowing into them. Your attention had already moved on, ghost-like, to dwell in a hollow fantasy of your future success. You were only partially present at the scene of the climb. You were climbing in order to be

The massive roofs of the Obed, northeastern Tennessee. *Photo: Shullphoto*

finished climbing. Now that you are finished climbing, it is as if you never really climbed.

One of the first times I was conscious of really enjoying the journey occurred in Yosemite Valley. In 1984 I climbed El Capitan for the first time. Steve Petro and I had just spent four days climbing *Zodiac*. We were worn out after the climb and now faced the job of dragging all our gear and ourselves down to the valley floor. Walking down the shoulder of El Cap to the East Ledges and doing the rappels with heavy haul sacks and ropes biting into our shoulders and hips, our attention wandered to the future, that soon-to-be-experienced time when we'd be down, showered, and relaxing.

As I walked the last mile or so, I had a conscious realization that this experience, so rich and rewarding, was almost over. It would then drift into memory and slowly fade away. I realized then I wanted to feel all the pain, discomfort, and everything that was happening at the moment. I wanted to feel it fully without trying to escape it. The experience would be over all too soon, and I wanted to feel it in its entirety.

Thinking of a future destination, when I'd be pain-free and comfortable, didn't change the fact that I was currently in pain. By feeling the discomfort and the weariness, my full attention remained in the moment. I still remember the experience vividly, even the descent. By staying in the discomfort of the moment, my experience was much richer, and I can actually relate that I enjoyed that suffering.

Many climbers have had experiences like this at the end of long, drawn-out challenges. They realize they've been on a great adventure which is almost over. The art of the warrior Journey process is to stay in this mindset even during a five-minute challenge.

Grace Under Pressure and Playing for Keeps

The Journey mindset focuses attention in the present. To climb at our greatest potential we need all our attention focused on the climbing. We can't squander it on the future. This is easier said than done. The risk zone is uncomfortable, and we are in the habit of escaping discomfort. What we say in the heat of the moment, such as, "If I could just get to that hold …" betrays the mindset: our attention is slipping out of the journey toward a destination.

Stop the tendency to let your attention move from one comfort zone to the next. Such an approach will make your effort jerky, halting, and

Forget the top. Just be there. *Photo: Jeff Achey*

wasteful of energy. Instead, be fluid and flexible. Climb continuously, with unbending intent, leaving no time to latch onto fear and doubt.

Discomfort, a sense of chaos, fight-or-flight responses—these characterize a typical climber's experience in the risk zone. The warrior's task is to enter the risk so knowingly and so fully that he can embrace the stressful conditions and not fight them. In the risk zone you will naturally experience a tension between opposites: between the desire to rest and the desire to exercise your power; between the desire to emerge at the top of the challenge and the desire to be tested. Hold the tension. Find comfort in the chaos. Break the habit of wanting to escape a demanding situation as quickly as possible. Adopt an attitude of appreciation toward the challenge and the learning. Set goals that involve the journey and the effort rather than the destination and the redpoint. The goal shouldn't be to redpoint a climb but to stay focused on the effort so that a redpoint ascent will manifest. You'll find that your climbing makes a lot more sense. And it's more fun.

The truth that his time on earth is limited helps the warrior appreciate the moment. The warrior lets death be his advisor. This may sound ominous, but it helps you take life seriously. It is simply a no-nonsense reminder that each moment matters. In the face of our mortality, externally derived values and the petty ways of the Ego seem ridiculous. Being mindful that we will inevitably die, we don't cling to petty destinations. Everything external will one day be taken from us, so, in a sense, we have nothing to lose. Death advises us to always use attention on what is important: learning and growth.

Death, however, does not advise us to be reckless. Our time on earth is precious. We don't want to foolishly squander any portion of it. There is no practice run. If we're facing a challenge we believe in, then we'll give it 100-percent attention. The warrior strives to undertake each act as if it is his last battle on earth.

The Journey process is the Rock Warrior's way of keeping attention in the present moment and being comfortable there, regardless of how stressful and chaotic the situation. His comfort comes from being in touch with his deepest values: learning from experiences, loving life, and increasing his personal power. Physically, he deals with the chaos of challenging climbing by using creative rests, holding on loosely, pacing, staying in balance, and expressing joy in giving effort. These things focus attention on finding comfort in the risk. If his attention wanders up the climb toward a destination, then he reminds himself of his intention to act, not to think about having acted. He resolutely brings his attention back to the task at hand. If he's at a loss for what to do, he does not lapse into a sense of impasse. He focuses on possibilities, giving himself the performance cue, "What now?" This is a direct question asked of his intuitive channels, which then home in on the opportunities in the situation.

Although it's helpful to break down experience into preparation, transition, and action, the Rock Warrior's path is really more holistic. Each task of preparation is part of the larger Journey. We may not prepare for action perfectly every time, but we acknowledge this as part of the warrior's path. We ruthlessly examine our motivation from the Witness position. We keep our attention on the process and learn from our experiences. We don't lie to ourselves about our efforts and our performances, nor do we punish ourselves. As we understand ourselves better, our power increases. Our mindset when we climb is no longer like a disobedient dog, always blundering into trouble and then cowering in guilt or fear of punishment. It becomes an instrument of power. The action word for the Journey process is **Attention**. Apply attention now, in the moment, in every step of the journey.

Conclusion

Peter Croft, Mark Wilford, and John Bachar are three of the most masterful climbers I know when it comes to risky or dangerous climbing. Recently I asked them why they are able to deal with fear while so many other climbers are not. You know what they told me? Basically, they said they didn't know why, or they hadn't thought about it very much. When I heard that, I was glad I had written this book. I've thought about this question often, and tested my answers on the rock. Mental training need not be intangible and vague; it can be very simple, understandable, and practical. The Rock Warrior's Way philosophy is very pragmatic.

Whether Croft, Wilford, or Bachar know it or not, the thing that most helps them deal with fear is that they deeply love what they do. This is the foundation of the Rock Warrior's Way: love-based motivation. If you are strong in your love-based motivation you are already practicing the warrior processes whether or not you're conscious of it. When you love something, attention is automatically focused in the moment because there is no other place you'd rather be.

Springing directly from a love of what you do and a focus on the present is an alignment with learning. All living things, you included, are created, grow, and then die. Since you already have been created and aren't dead yet, you are most in harmony when you align yourself with the positive process in between—growth. You live in a dynamic world. If you are settling in to a rigid comfort zone, then you are dying—slowly, but still dying. To stay vibrant you need to engage life and take risks, not for the conquest of some elusive mountaintop or redpoint, but in order to learn and grow.

Value learning. It nourishes our growth. Learning is solving problem after problem, acting on one opportunity after another. You demonstrate that you value learning by keeping attention on those problems and opportunities. When you feel distracted or stressed, ask, "Is my attention focused on solving this problem?" or, "What is the opportunity for learning in this situation?" If attention isn't focused on solving the problem or acting on the opportunity, stop leaking that attention and use it impeccably to deal with whatever is at hand.

Just because the principle is simple doesn't mean it's easy to accomplish. We are all rife with limiting habits and ineffective beliefs. The Rock Warrior's Way isn't a destination that you struggle to attain. It's here, now. It is the struggle itself. This book lays out seven processes that help guide you on your path. To follow the Rock Warrior's Way means to decide to walk the path. Then, simply be observant and pay attention.

A warrior prepares for the risks he knows he'll be encountering. He uses attention to collect information about the risk, changing as much as possible of the unknown to the known. He knows that the Ego will try to sabotage his effort. He separates to the Witness position with sword in hand and slices off any dragon head the Ego raises. He centers himself so he is present for the upcoming challenge. He assesses the consequences and focuses on possibilities in the situation. Then he makes a decision, to take the risk or not. He transitions from preparation to action. If he decides to take the risk, he cuts off all possibilities of re-deciding, hesitating, or doubting and commits wholeheartedly to the effort. He sets an intention to take action and commits 100-percent to that intention. Once he's launched into the action phase, he knows he isn't in Kansas anymore. He's in a new realm, complete with unknown elements, unrealized potential, and magic. He expects to have doubts and fears arise in his consciousness. He dismisses these and stays with his intention to act.

As you walk the path, stay aligned with growth and learning. You are in a paradoxical situation because you will tend to be drawn to comfort, security, and "successes." But these cannot be attained directly. Only by focusing your attention into the moment and on the process, not on the outcome, can you arrive at the place you desire.

It's a very personal journey. It's your journey. You will find yourself at odds with the ways of the masses, whose lives are focused on striving for comfort and security. The Warrior's Way is a lonely journey and doesn't wait for respect or approval from others.

Reading this book will automatically improve your awareness. That's an important first step. It's the preparation phase. Ponder what you've read. Process it. Now, you face the transition phase. You face the choice.

Will you move forward into the challenge, or retreat to your comfort zone? Reach deep down within you and pull out the courage to walk the warrior's path. Decide to apply it wholeheartedly on the rocks.

Remember also, the Rock Warrior's Way is a way of balance and harmony and there is a life purpose behind it. The important things we want, redpoints included, are simply stepping-stones to living a more peaceful life. We want to be at peace with ourselves and be able to maintain that peace in the face of adversity. The ability to do that is the highest expression of the warrior's power.

Accept the journey. Be at peace in it. Watch it. When you can be at one with the difficulty and the chaos, then you transcend it. You simply walk your path, being observant, paying attention, learning and growing in your understanding of who you are and what is possible for you. Approached in the warrior's way, the rock will teach you.

Photo: Jeff Achey

Exercises

Introduction

1. Setting an Intention

Whatever you choose to practice, set an intention. In the climbing exercises below, set a conscious intention prior to leaving the ground. Your partner can help. Ask your belayer not to yell vague encouragement, such as, "Go for it!" or, "You can do it!" but rather to remind you of your specific intention.

By setting a specific intention you'll sharpen your focus and reduce the chance of falling into your habitual way of climbing. Setting an intention helps you stay on task for what you want to practice.

2. Visualization

Have you ever had a route that you really wanted to do and couldn't get out of your mind? When you went to sleep at night you saw yourself going through the moves? That's visualization. Visualization is a long-standing staple of mental training, used by athletes from Olympians to tennis amateurs. Essentially, it's nothing more than closing your eyes and mentally going through the activity you want to do, in the way you want to do it. Even if you don't consciously "visualize," you still have images in your brain that will strongly influence your performance. Most of these will be unconscious. They may include images of you becoming helplessly pumped or falling off the crux move. These images tend to bring about the reality. Likewise, images of you climbing effortlessly, in perfect balance, and of powering smoothly through crux moves, can create that reality. Your body responds to commands from the mind. By deliberately practicing visualization you choreograph the performance you want and ingrain it, not only in your mental realm but also in your physical body.

In your mind's eye, see yourself going through the moves flawlessly and precisely, as you want to do on the rock. Make the vision as realistic as possible, including tying into the rope, the sounds and smells of the environment, and the texture of the rock. These details will help the visualization match the actual event and "kick in" as you begin to climb.

Chapter 1, Becoming Conscious

1. **Meditation**

Meditation takes many forms. For our purposes, meditation means keeping your attention on your breathing and witnessing when thoughts carry your attention away from the breath. Your attention may go to sounds you hear or things you need to do later.

Meditation helps you identify the Witness position. You are not your thoughts; you are the observer of your thoughts. The Witness is the position from which you notice thoughts carrying your attention to other things in your environment. By identifying the Witness you give yourself a position of power from which to observe your thoughts. Then, you can consciously choose whether or not to act on any given thought.

2. **STOP**

This exercise comes from George Gurdjieff, the Russian author on warriorship. It's a simple exercise: you say "STOP!" when you catch yourself in a habit.

If you can stop the habit, you prove that you have conscious control of your behavior; if you can't stop, you are unconscious and functioning on "automatic," a slave to the habit. For example, if you habitually become defensive when corrected by someone, say, "STOP!" Can you stop defending yourself?

The purpose of the exercise is to check your consciousness of habits, and help break them. By saying "STOP!" you give yourself a moment of consciousness to stop acting out the habit.

3. **Delay and Dissociate**

Setup: Choose a route that is outside your comfort zone. If you've done lead climbing then it's best to do this exercise on lead. Climb to the point where you think falling is inevitable. Habitual thoughts will arise, such as to down-climb or to grab a draw. At the moment of truth, you'll ... wait.

Set the intention: to delay acting out a habit. Recognize before you start up the route that as you get stressed, "comfort" thoughts will come up. Perhaps you're in the habit of telling yourself that you must grab a draw, say "Take," or in some other way escape the discomfort of the effort. Welcome these thoughts. When they arise, simply delay acting on them. Don't down-climb, don't grab a draw, don't *do* anything. Simply hold on to the holds and stay where you are.

Next, begin "dissociating" from your habitual flow of actions. By delaying, you've broken the one-two momentum of the habit. Then, further break down the habit by talking about it and making it conscious. Talk to yourself. Call yourself by name: "Okay Arno, you just thought about grabbing the draw. You may still grab it, but for now you'll delay." While you delay you can make a move up or down or reposition your body. Delay or do anything that is different than what you habitually do. Once you've broken the chain of actions that form a habit, you can finish the exercise with any non-habitual action. Do something that feels a little bold. Say, "Give me two feet of slack!" rather than "Take!"—then jump off. Or, keep climbing and go for the next rest. Purposely slap for a useless hold and force a fall. It doesn't matter what you do, as long as it's non-habitual.

Delaying and dissociating help you move to the Witness position. From the Witness position you are able to break the habitual cycle of reacting to limiting thoughts.

4. Foreign Affairs

Setup: Put yourself in a climbing situation that you normally avoid or have never considered. The situation should make you extremely uncomfortable—it should feel *foreign*. For example, get on a climb and don't take your chalk bag. Or, climb in shoes that are too large. If you are a "strength" climber, get on a delicate slab climb.

Your goal is to produce an emotional reaction to the stressful situation. See if you react—by becoming frustrated, angry, or blaming something such as weak forearms. These type reactions indicate unconsciousness.

Set the intention: to observe these limiting behaviors.

This exercise helps you subdue your Ego and gain self-knowledge. Your Ego thrives by getting on routes where you have a significant chance of reaching the top. Observe when you get frustrated, angry, or react—all manifestations of the Ego not getting what it wants. Once you observe these limiting reactions and leaks of attention, you can plug them by stopping that behavior.

5. Self Stalking

Videotape yourself on a route at your limit. Climb as you normally do without changing anything. Then watch the video, noting your technique, body language, etc. Then, watch it again, this time recalling the inner dialogue you had at each point during the climb. Was your self-talk limiting or empowering? Can you see any effects that your self-talk had on your climbing?

Watching yourself on video is a great way to separate yourself from your performance. You are able to see your performance more objectively because you are seeing it as others would, separate from the subjective feelings of effort.

Chapter 2, Life is Subtle

1. Place/Push

Setup: Choose a route that is easy for you, either toprope or lead.

Set the intention: to climb by pushing with both legs. As you climb this way, push your hips up and in, close to the rock. Place/Push improves your consciousness of using your body to climb efficiently. It also creates a more positive posture, a more balanced style, and generates confidence.

2. Rock Meditation

This exercise is great to include in your warm-up.

Setup: Choose a route that is easy for you, either toprope or lead.

Set the intention: to climb slowly and pay attention to how you are climbing. Use precise footwork, climb and breathe continuously, push with both legs, and focus on balance.

By climbing efficiently and fluidly on easier routes you'll set a tone for the day that will continue through your later efforts on harder routes.

3. P-C-O

This is a written exercise. Answer each of these similar-sounding questions, in the order given:

What is the biggest problem you have with improving your climbing performance?

A:_____

_____.

What is the biggest challenge you have with improving your climbing performance?

A:_____

_____.

What is the biggest opportunity you have with improving your climbing performance?

A:_____

_____.

These questions are the same except for a single change: the words problem/challenge/opportunity. Your answers, however, may be revealing. When you see "improving your climbing performance" as a *problem*, your answer will show an avoidance orientation and you'll state the situation passively—for example, "I'm afraid of falling."

If you replace *problem* with *challenge* when framing the question, your answer will necessarily imply action: "My biggest challenge is to overcome my fear of falling." Even though you're talking about the same situation, your thought process is more love-based and you've got the beginnings of a plan.

Finally, if you replace *challenge* with *opportunity*, your answer becomes even more action-oriented and love-based. For example: "I have the chance to go out, practice some falls, and get over my falling fears." By using *opportunity* in the question, you generate an answer that helps you engage the situation and actively improve your performance. This is where you want to be. This is love-based motivation. You can use this three-part experiment for any performance-related question.

4. Deliberate Breathing

Setup: Choose a route that is easy for you, either toprope or lead.

Set the intention: to breathe deliberately. As you climb, simply focus on breathing continuously. With each breath, force the air out with your abdominal muscles and blow it audibly out of your mouth. By doing this you hear and feel that you are breathing continuously and not holding your breath. Your inhalation will become automatic and the breath cycle longer and deeper.

Breathing continuously and deliberately helps you stay in the process and reduces fears and anxieties.

5. Soft-Eyes Focus

Soft-eyes will make you more receptive and attentive to your surroundings.

Setup: Choose a route that is easy for you, either toprope or lead. As you climb, don't focus on any one hold, feature, or body part. You will see everything in your peripheral vision as well as what's right in front of you.

Set the intention: to spread out your visual attention so that it covers the whole field of view.

Normal visual focuses attention on a small part of your surroundings. Your conscious mind is isolating parts of the environment and homing in on them. By not focusing on any one thing in your field of view you spread out your attention. Soft-eyes focus gives equal value to all things, enabling you to obtain more complete information from the situation. Information can be picked up by your subconscious and incorporated into your climbing effort.

6. Left/Right Breathing

You may have heard of left-brain, right-brain research. Studies have shown that the two hemispheres of your cerebral cortex specialize in different kinds of jobs. The left brain is more analytical, logical, detail-oriented, sequential, and thinks in terms of objects. The right brain is more intuitive, creative, imaginative, and thinks in terms of relationships. Figuring out sequences and rests while working a route is a typical left-brain dominated activity. "Going with the flow" during an on-sight is more right-brained. The right brain is responsible for your connection to what, in this book, I've called the subconscious mind.

During the day your brain alternates dominance between left and right hemispheres and this dominance manifests itself in your breathing. Approximately every two hours the dominance switches. When the right brain is dominant, you breathe primarily through your left nostril because the right brain operates the left side of the body, and vice versa.

The Left/Right Breathing exercise helps you intentionally balance the hemispheres of your brain. First, inhale through your right nostril while holding your left nostril closed. Exhale through your left nostril while holding your right nostril closed. Repeat three times, and then switch sides.

Chapter 3, Accepting Responsibility

1. Describing Objectively

This exercise involves describing a climbing situation as if you were a scientist. Described objectively, a route will sound the same regardless of who describes it because an objective description has nothing to do with ability. This means the description won't include subjective words such as good, bad, hard, easy, reachy, pumpy, etc. Have your belayer also describe the route and see if your descriptions are similar. Then look for subjective elements in your description and eliminate them. Your goal is to gather information about the situation in order to see it as clearly as possible, without subjectivity or illusions.

You can do this exercise for various parts of a climbing situation, including:

A) The route. Describe the angle, type of rock, size of edges, spacing of protection, features, etc.

B) Your performance. Once you've climbed, describe your balance, your breathing, how well you stayed with your intention, etc.

2. Shirking Observation

As you become more familiar with the Rock Warrior's Way approach to risk-taking, you'll gain awareness of self-limiting and self-empowering talk. To refine this awareness, notice how self-limiting talk occurs at the climbing areas you frequent. Listen to other climbers. Do they become frustrated, angry, say they suck, make excuses about weak forearms, etc.? Observing other climbers' self-limiting talk helps you eliminate similar habits in yourself.

Chapter 4, Giving

1. Giving a Skill

Setup: Choose a challenging route to climb. Then, identify specifically what will challenge you. Identify what strength, skill, talent, or experience you have that will help you deal with the specific challenge on the route.

Set the intention: to **give** the skill you've identified as you climb the route. Stay focused on giving that skill to the effort.

After the climb, reflect on how you felt and how you performed. Did you stay with your intention? Did you stay focused and discover that the climb was possible or not as difficult as previously thought?

2. Metaphor Focus

This exercise helps identify how you represent potentially stressful climbing situations to yourself. I've modified this exercise from a similar exercise that Anthony Robbins teaches. It begins with a free association, analyzes the results, and then explores a possible new association.

Three climbing situations that typically cause stress are falling, leading trad, and climbing at one's limit. (You can substitute another situation if you have one that causes you more stress.) The Metaphor Focus exercise creates metaphors for these situations.

Begin with the statement, "Falling is ..." and then fill in the blank with a word or words that come to mind. When you think of falling, what words come into your head? A possible *metaphor* might be: "death," or "failure," or "flying." The words you choose are how you metaphorically represent falling to yourself.

Let's say you choose "death." The second part of the exercise asks, "If falling is death, then what does that mean to me?" The last part of the exercise creates a new metaphor. Here's a template for the exercise:

Falling is _____.

Leading trad is _____.

Climbing at my limit is_____.

Now, using the metaphor that you've determined above, answer these questions:

If falling is _____, then what does that mean to me?
A:_____.

If leading trad is _____, then what does that mean to me?
A:_____.

If climbing at my limit is _____, then what does that mean to me?
A:_____.

Now, change your metaphors to more empowering ones. What metaphor would be more empowering than the one you used? *Clue: use a word or words that focus on learning.*

Falling is _____.

Leading trad is _____.

Climbing at my limit is_____.

This exercise builds awareness of how you represent stressful situations to yourself. If you represent them as something to avoid, then you will resist engaging them. If you consciously create an empowering metaphor, you will tend to respond in an empowered way.

3. Imaging the Process

I've noticed that climbers who naturally perform strongly—close to their potential—tend to image the process of a climb rather than the result. They see challenges as being within their ability because they see them made up of processes that are within their ability. For example, a climber wants to climb a 5.11 finger crack that is at his limit. He doesn't image the destination of doing an on-sight or redpoint, but rather images the components that will lead to an on-sight or redpoint. He images placing pro, doing finger jams, pacing himself, climbing efficiently, etc.—all things he knows how to do. Therefore he images himself rising to the challenge and using his abilities.

Find a route that will be challenging for you. Look for the components that will be required to climb the route. Image your ability to apply yourself to these components. After practicing this exercise on several routes, you will find that you are aware of many more routes that are possible for you. You've probably been walking past these routes year after year, thinking they were beyond your ability.

Chapter 5, Choices

1. The Lunge

This exercise helps develop your ability to commit. The exercise is simple: instead of climbing statically, you'll practice lunging or leaping for holds. Lunges are particularly committing moves, since if you miss the hold you're lunging for, or don't grab it well, then you will fall. You can't just reach up and feel around—you need to commit. That's the point of the exercise.

You can do the exercise on the rock, on boulders, on toprope, or even on lead, but practicing lunging is easiest in a climbing gym. You have many choices of holds, close to the ground, and you can safely fall onto the padded floor.

Setup: First, find an opportunity for a lunge. The classic lunge involves a very long, dynamic reach past a holdless section, but you can invent a fine lunge simply by ignoring intermediate holds. It's possible to lunge on almost any reachy move, even one that you could also do statically, but for this exercise it's better to find a move that you can only do by lunging, using starting holds that are hard to hold onto if you miss your target. Your goal is to invent a move that requires a feeling of 100-percent commitment to accomplish. This way you won't be able to "cheat." You'll only make the move if you fully commit to flying, and if you miss you'll fall. (Note: After only a little practice you'll find you need to invent longer lunges for yourself in order to demand that feeling of 100-percent commitment. You're learning a powerful climbing skill, which you can use on the rock, but that's not the main purpose of this exercise!)

Set the intention: to commit 100-percent to the lunge. Focus your attention on creating an explosive, confident, 100-percent effort.

To increase the commitment required, lunge with both hands at the same time. Do a two-handed lunge on a vertical wall, starting in a crouched position and using large footholds. The leg power you can generate this way allows huge lunges, even if your upper-body strength is limited. Another variation involves lunging with both hands at the same time, to two different target holds. (Tip: use "soft-eyes focus" when doing this variation.)

When you lunge, you must commit to the move in order to make it through. If you are tentative, you'll fall. Lunging builds confidence and gives you a concrete, one-move example of what 100-percent commitment feels like.

2. **Appropriate Risk Assessment**

This is a variation of Describing Objectively (Chapter 3 Exercises). Risk assessment is a craft requiring clear thinking and thoroughness. When facing an intimidating crux, many climbers simply ask themselves,

"Will I fall or not?" Answering this question gives you no information, and in fact sets you up to use a haphazard guess to guide your actions. This exercise gives you an outline for more appropriate risk assessment.

Setup: Find a route on which you will have to risk a fall. Ideally, find a route where you can pause restfully below the potential fall section, so you can go through the exercise without rushing or getting pumped.

Your goal is to decide whether or not a risk is appropriate for you. Do this by assessing the fall consequences and comparing these to your experience with similar consequences. Remember that you don't assess the consequences by figuring out whether or not you will fall. Rather, you understand that a fall is always possible and you weigh the fall consequences against your experience with responding to such consequences. *Set the intention*: to assess the risk thoroughly and objectively.

A) Assess the fall consequence. Ask these questions: "How far is the pro spaced? Is the climbing in line with the pro? Where will I end up if I do take a fall? How far will the fall be? Are there any ledges? Is the route overhanging or slabby? Will the fall be straight down or will I pendulum?"

B) Assess your experience with falls of the type you are considering. Ask, "How much experience do I have with this kind of fall consequence?" Compare the potential fall with other falls you've taken. Is it similar? What, exactly, are the differences? Are these differences incremental or great? Can you mentally bridge the gap between falls you've taken and the fall you're assessing, and can you envision how to take the fall with a reasonable margin of safety? How did you respond to falls in the past? How will your planned response to this fall differ from your past responses to similar falls?

C) Decide whether or not to take the risk. Remember, the point of this exercise is not necessarily to take the risk, but to practice the assessment method and make an appropriate choice. If the type of fall you're considering is far beyond your experience, then the risk is probably not appropriate for you. Find a route with a more familiar fall consequence or do some intentional falling practice (see next exercise) and gain experience before taking on the risk.

By systematically assessing consequences and your experience, you will commit to risks that are more appropriate for you and minimize the chances of injury.

3. Falling Practice

Practicing falling helps take the falling experience out of the unknown and makes it part of the normal climbing process. **Warning: falling can be dangerous!** Choose your fall zones wisely, and practice in small, gradual steps. Make sure you accept responsibility for how you choose to practice.

The fall-practice zone should not have any protruding ledges and should have good bolts or several pieces of trad pro for protection. The failure of any single piece should not result in an unacceptably dangerous fall. In the beginning of your practice, choose a fall zone that is slightly overhanging to help reduce possibility of injury. Then, as you gain experience, you can practice other falling situations, such as those on vertical rock or with slightly swinging falls. Have plenty of rope in the system—at least thirty feet of rope between you and your belayer—to absorb the fall force. The rope will stretch during your practice session, so, after a few falls, hang on a piece of pro and let the rope regain its shape and length.

Maintain proper form as you practice falling. Proper form includes keeping arms and legs slightly bent, with arms out in front at chest height so you can respond to the impact. Don't grab the rope. Step off gently rather than jumping out and back, which can cause you to slam into the wall. Breathe continuously and stay relaxed.

Recommended sample of graduated falling practice:

A) Toprope. Begin falling practice on toprope. First, climb up a ways, then simply let go and hang on the rope. Swing to the left and to the right, shuffling or even running back and forth across the rock. Become comfortable with being unattached to the rock and trusting the system. Next, with a clear zone beneath you, ask for a few feet of slack and jump. Repeat with a little more slack. Pay attention to your form as you practice.

B) Lead falls. Begin this step by taking falls right at your protection point. This is like a toprope fall; you'll only fall as much as the rope stretches. After you are comfortable with this, climb up one move and take a fall. Continue in small increments, one or two moves up at a time. Practice several times at each increment until you're comfortable increasing the fall distance. Becoming comfortable with falls of twenty feet will prepare you quite well for the fall consequence on most sport climbs. Remember, however, that practicing falling can be dangerous. Choose your fall zone wisely!

C) Diagonal falls. Not all routes are straight, and neither are the falls that can result from them. Once you gain some falling savvy you may want to gain experience with falls that include a swing or pendulum.

If you have some control over your fall, you can reduce dangerous swings by the way you detach from the rock. To practice this technique, climb diagonally away from your protection point for a few feet, and then jump off in the direction of your last piece of pro. Notice how the jump anticipates the direction you would swing when the rope comes taut and reduces or eliminates your pendulum across the wall. Notice how your trajectory changes with various jump tactics and distances from your protection point.

Note: By practicing falling you help separate real concerns from phantom fear and improve your understanding of the consequences. You learn how to fall properly, thus minimizing, but not eliminating, the chance of injury on a "routine" fall.

Any fall can hurt you, but there are some routes with potential falls that will cause injury or death. On these routes it's important to NOT push yourself past the point of no return and thereby take a fall. This may seem obvious but I feel it's important to emphasize it. *A fall can happen at any time.* Don't go on "R" (runout) or "X" (ground-fall potential) routes thinking that a fall can't happen. Don't fool yourself thinking that just because it's not a good idea to fall that you won't fall. Holds could break, you can slip, or you could pump out. Learning about falling includes learning how to recognize when falling will cause injury or death. Decide beforehand if you're entering a risk that you are willing to take, and pay attention. Know when it's time to back down and get off the route.

Chapter 6, Listening

1. **Liar, Liar**

Many climbers "decide" to fall when they are convinced by their conscious mind that they can't continue climbing. Basically, they don't give 100-percent; they give up. We tend to give up when our discomfort becomes "too much to bear." Seeking comfort, our conscious minds lie to us, and decide for us to fall.

Setup: Find a route that will be challenging for you, either an unknown route at or above your maximum current on-sight grade, or a redpoint project you are working on. It's best to do this exercise on lead rather than on toprope. Make sure the route has fall consequences that you have some experience with; you will very likely be falling so you want to minimize the chance of injury.

Set the intention: Instead of "deciding" to fall, intend to climb until you fall. In other words, if your conscious mind is convinced that you are about to fall, continue climbing anyway. Do the next move instead of "deciding" to fall. Focus all your attention on that next move—and the one after that if you find yourself still on the rock—and don't let your attention be distracted by the lies of your conscious mind.

As you enter the risk zone, a crux of some sort, expect your conscious mind to create "comfort" thoughts. Examples include: "I'm too pumped to continue," "The hold is too small for me to pull on," "The fall is too scary," "I need to grab the draw," or "I had better down-climb and rest on the bolt." Recognize that these thoughts are not true representations of whether or not you can continue climbing. When you are in the risk zone, acting out the risk, the conscious mind is a liar. It will try to pull you back into its realm: the comfort zone. Recognize "comfort" thoughts and remind yourself of your intention: to commit forward into the climbing.

By making the next move anyway you stay with your intention to climb and therefore make your intention more unbending. Doing this will help you break through the mental barriers of the conscious mind.

2. Continuous Climbing

This is an intuitive climbing exercise. By setting your intention on constantly moving your arms and legs, you'll be forced to respond to intuitive signals and disengage from conscious thinking.

Setup: Choose a route that is easy for you. Climb on toprope, to keep your task as simple as possible.

Set the intention: to climb with continuous movement without stopping to rest or think. Climbing rapidly will help you minimize conscious thought, but keep your focus on continuous movement rather than speed. When you can do this exercise on easy routes, move on to harder routes until you are able to climb continuously near or at your limit.

You can do many variations of this basic exercise.

A) In the gym, find an area that has numerous holds and climb continuously and rapidly within a ten- or fifteen-foot circle. Moving one limb at a time, begin climbing up, down, sideways, and around in small circles.

B) Do the exercise while leading sport climbs. Move continuously, whether climbing, placing draws, or clipping the rope. Integrate your movements, perhaps placing a draw with one hand, climbing up a move, and then clipping the rope with the other hand.

C) Do the exercise on trad leads that are easy for you. Incorporate the movements of placing protection into your continuous movement. Integrate the climbing moves and the placing of protection moves, for example holding on with your right hand to remove a piece of gear from your rack and place it, then moving up to a higher left handhold to slip a runner off your right shoulder. Continuous movement doesn't mean you should mindlessly "plug and chug." If a protection piece doesn't fit well, remove it and place a quality piece. Simply concentrate on making motions continuously rather than stalling out and thinking too much. Once you master this skill on easy routes, move on to harder trad leads, making sure you safeguard your effort by focusing attention on setting quality placements.

3. The Eyes Have It

This exercise is a spin-off of Continuous Climbing and is designed to increase your awareness of your body's intuitive knowledge of how to move without your conscious involvement. It helps show that the conscious mind doesn't have to think everything through in order for you to climb well.

Setup: Pick a route that is easy for you, one on which you can move freely without too much effort or thought about sequences. Climbing on toprope works well for this exercise because it allows you to move continuously. As you begin climbing, separate yourself from your climbing effort and observe yourself from the Witness position. Observe how your eyes automatically direct the movements of your arms and legs. Keep your awareness separate from the climbing and observe how your eyes are directing your movements. You will automatically look in the direction where a hand or foot needs to move to maintain balance.

Nature moves toward being in harmony and balance. Your intuition, through your eyes, directs you toward harmony. Trust in this process. Trust that your body knows how to move without you having to consciously tell it how to move.

There is nothing unusual about your eyes looking in a direction to maintain balance. It's becoming conscious of this fact that awakens your power.

Set the intention: to separate from the effort, move to the Witness position, and observe how your eyes direct your movements.

A sharpened version of this exercise is called **No Second Guessing**. Follow your eyes and use the first hold you grab or put your foot on. If the hold isn't as large or as positive as you expected, use it anyway. Many times the first hold is the most effective one, even if it doesn't offer the most security.

4. Observing Controlling Behavior

This exercise is similar to the observing exercise in the Accepting Responsibility process. As you become more familiar with the Rock Warrior's Way approach you'll gain awareness of controlling behavior. Your Ego will try to conceal your own controlling behavior from you, but it has no problem allowing you to see it in others. Observe the behaviors in others, and then use what you've observed to help identify the same behaviors in yourself.

When you go climbing, observe how other climbers climb. Do they fall into controlling behaviors such as stopping, holding their breath, resisting falling, over-gripping, down-climbing, or grabbing a draw? Does it help their effort?

Controlling behaviors prevent you from committing 100-percent forward and climbing continuously. Observing other climbers' controlling behaviors will help you see them in yourself and strengthen your resolve to eliminate them.

Chapter 7, The Journey

1. Comfortable Chaos

The essence of the Journey process is to be present with the chaos of the risk situation without trying to escape it. This exercise anticipates and simplifies the chaos, allowing you to find a feeling of comfort in it.

Setup: Find a route that will challenge you in a specific way. Determine what it is about the route that will challenge you. Be specific. Example: On a smooth, less-than-vertical route, you'll be challenged by feeling insecure because the holds are small and you may pop off at any moment. Or, on an overhanging jug route you'll be challenged by the pump factor. Ask friends or other climbers to direct you toward the kind of challenge you want to work on, but don't obtain specific, move-by-move information. You want to know what kind of chaos to prepare for, yet retain a strong sense of the unknown as you begin.

Next, anticipate what you can do to find comfort in the risk. Example: On the smooth, less-than-vertical route you can focus on staying in balance, making crisp and decisive step-ups, taking short steps, trusting small holds, and pushing with both legs. On the overhanging jug route you can focus on hanging straight-armed between moves, holding on loosely by relaxing your grip, climbing dynamically, using heel-hooks, doing drop-knees, or any other arm-saving leg techniques, and climbing deliberately between the rests. Regardless of what specific techniques you decide will aid your effort, focus on those skills that will create a degree of comfort in the chaos of the risk zone.

Set the intention: to use known techniques to find comfort in the chaos. After the effort, see how well you stayed with your intention. Did your attention stay on employing your skills, or did it stray to thoughts of escaping the risk?

2. Directed Climbing

Here, a partner helps create climbing chaos by choosing moves for you. In this exercise, it's almost impossible to adopt a destination focus because you never know where you'll be directed next.

Setup: This exercise is best done in a bouldering cave at a climbing gym. Find a section of wall where you can stay on for a dozen moves or more while becoming increasingly pumped. You'll need a partner, and a pointer such as a broomstick. Get on the wall, and have your partner point to the next handhold for you to grab or foothold to step on. Let your partner direct you to climb up, to stop, to climb down, go sideways, or climb in any manner that will keep you uncertain of what will happen next. Your partner should be able to notice when you are getting pumped so he can direct you to a rest or to larger handholds to recover. Then he can direct you to climb again. Continue the exercise until you fall off. When someone else directs your climbing, the destination is taken away. You have no choice but to focus on the journey, be in the moment, and find efficient ways to move.

Set the intention: to listen to who is directing your climbing and to climb efficiently.

Putting It All Together
The Rock Warrior's Way Approach

When you put all of your warrior skills together, you create a style for taking risks. A "risk" in climbing is a single-effort event that may be an entire climb, but often is only part of a climb. It's effective to envision a risk as the distance you need to climb before you'll get a chance for a new preparation phase. For a sustained sport-climbing redpoint, this may be the entire climb. On a sport climbing on-sight, the risk may be to climb to the next bolt or to a rest. A trad-climbing risk might be the distance from your current stance to the next rest. Find routes that will challenge you and that have a certain level of unknown.

Set the intention: to apply the complete Rock Warrior's Way approach, as outlined below.

Preparation Phase

1. *Observe leaks of attention.* From the Witness position observe if you are leaking attention into phantom fear or what others will think of your performance, etc.

2. *Center yourself* by doing a strong exhalation, shaking your face to remove any grimace, checking your posture by bringing your hips in close to the rock, and then breathing calmly. Talk to yourself by saying, "Calm down, breathe, shake out, regain," etc.

3. *Accept the consequences.* Discover the details about the risk you're facing. Look up to see where the risk will end—the next pro or rest. Where will you end up if you fall? In this stage, dispel all illusions and accept the situation as it is. This is not the time to say "yes" to the risk. Simply accept exactly what it is that you're considering, both the effort and the fall consequence.

4. *Focus on possibilities* and what you can do to climb through the risk. For on-sighting: Think of general possibilities, such as the types of holds and sequences. For redpoints: You already know the sequence, so create an image that the climbing is possible for you.

Transition Phase

5. *Commit* to taking the risk or not. There are only two possible out-comes: you climb through or you fall. You assessed the fall conse-quence in step three, which means you no longer wish the consequence

to be different or less severe. In Choices, you weigh the fall consequence against your experience of responding to those consequences. Now, decide whether or not to take the risk. If you can accept both outcomes, and you choose to take the risk, then you are ready to transition to the action phase. *Set the intention*: to commit forward to climbing. Don't go before you are ready, but when you go, go!

Action Phase

6. *Trust in the process* by climbing and breathing continuously. By climbing this way you maintain your momentum. You are in the risk now, focusing forward 100-percent. Your conscious mind, however, will try to pull you back into the comfort zone. Expect your conscious mind to create "comfort" thoughts and realize they are not true representations of your ability. Remind yourself to stay with your intention to commit forward to climbing.

7. *Keep attention in the moment* by looking for comfort in the risk rather than at some destination. Don't let your attention stray to the top of the climb, to the next rest, or to your last pro. You'll either get there or you won't. Find comfort in the chaos by staying balanced, relaxing your grip, and pacing yourself well. Relish the journey.

PREPARATION PHASE
1. Observe yourself from the Witness position.
2. Center yourself with a strong exhalation, shake your face, position body positively, and talk to yourself.
3. Look up for the next pro placement. Look down to check out the fall consequence. "Where will I end up should I fall before I reach the next pro/rest?"
4. Look up for possibilities for climbing the risk.

TRANSITION PHASE
5. Be decisive. When you go, go! Set an intention to commit forward to climbing.

ACTION PHASE
6. Climb and breathe continuously.
7. Look for comfort in the risk.

The warrior's path is seldom easy, but it's always interesting.
Photo: Jeff Achey

Glossary

5.8, 5.10, 5.13, etc.: The numbers of an open-ended difficulty-rating system for rock climbing, ranging from 5.0 (easiest) to 5.15 (most difficult). Originally, ratings were intended to follow a decimal system, but when routes more difficult than 5.9 were done, the decimal concept was modified and grades of 5.10 and 5.11 were added. The prefix "5" refers to "5th class" climbing; the system also includes classes 1, 2, 3, and 4, indicating progressively more rugged and exposed scrambling.

Bolt: A permanent protection point consisting of a steel stud set into a small hole drilled in the rock and fitted with a hanger for clipping.

Bouldering: Free climbing without a rope, generally on boulders but also in a climbing gym or along the base of a larger cliff, close enough to the ground so that a fall is not likely to result in injury.

Cam: Common term for a spring-loaded rock-climbing protection device. Examples include Friends, Camalots, **TCUs**.

Chock: A rock-climbing protection device consisting of a wedge-, hex-, or otherwise-shaped piece of metal, slung with a cord or thin cable, that can be slotted into a widening or irregularity in a fissure in the rock. The various sizes of chocks fit cracks from approximately 1/8 inch to four inches. Other names for chocks include nuts, stoppers, hexes, wedges, wires (for small, cabled chocks).

Crux: The most difficult part of a climbing route.

Dihedral: A section of cliff where two planes of rock meet at an angle, forming a feature similar in appearance to the corner of a room. Dihedrals may also be acute or obtuse, overhanging or low-angle.

Free climbing: Climbing a section of rock without physical aid from ropes or climbing gear. The rope and gear may be used for protection, but not for progress or resting. There are many sub-categories of free climbing, including bouldering, free soloing, toproping, on-sighting, and redpointing.

Free soloing: Free climbing without a rope, high enough off the ground so that a fall would result in very serious injury or death.

Jamming: A technique for climbing cracks that involves wedging various body parts into the fissure.

Layback: A crack-climbing technique often used in corner-cracks (**dihedrals**). The climber grasps the edge of the crack, leans back, and moves upward by "walking" the feet up the opposing wall and advancing the hands up the crack.

Nut: A rock-climbing protection device; see **Chock**.

On-sighting: Ascending a route on your first effort. You climb from the bottom to the top, placing or clipping protection as you go. You see it and climb it, first go—no foreknowledge of moves or holds, no falls, no working the route.

Pro: Short for protection. Examples include bolts and quickdraws for sport routes; cams, wedges, slings, etc. for trad routes.

Redpoint: Leading a climb from the bottom to the top, placing pro (and/or clipping fixed pro) as you go, without hanging or pulling on any protection. Redpointing usually refers to an ascent that is relatively difficult for the climber, and thus not accomplished "on-sight." Climbers may work a route, hanging and resting on pro to figure out moves, then do a redpoint effort. Very challenging redpoints may take days and even years of effort to accomplish.

Runout: The distance between protection points, especially when it is long. Also, the act of climbing between said points.

Slab: A smooth, low-angle rock face usually climbed using very small holds and friction.

Sport climbing: Climbing on routes that are protected only by bolts. Sport routes generally employ closely spaced bolts to protect face climbing on steep slabs or vertical to overhanging faces.

Take: A rope command used by the climber to request that the belay rope be held tight and his weight held by the belayer.

TCU: Acronym for "three-cam unit." Generally used to indicate any very small **Cam,** regardless of the number of cams the device has. TCUs fit cracks from approximately 1/4 to 3/4 inches wide.

Trad climbing: Short for traditional climbing. This type of climbing generally follows "lines of weakness" in the rock, such as cracks or flakes, into which one places chocks or camming devices for protection. Trad routes often involve face climbing, and may or may not employ protection bolts, which will usually be more widely spaced than on sport routes. Some trad routes (for example, most crack routes) have plenty of available protection while others may require long runouts between protection points.

Reading List

Books

Blanton, W. Brad, *Radical Honesty*, New York, NY: Dell Publishing, 1994. Honesty is the cornerstone of the Accepting Responsibility process. Dr. Blanton digs deep into scrupulous honesty.

Castaneda, Carlos, *Tales of Power*, New York, NY: Simon and Schuster, 1974. I've found all the Castaneda books fascinating and profound. This and the following two titles are richly filled with don Juan's teachings.

Castaneda, Carlos, *The Fire from Within*, New York, NY: Simon and Schuster, 1985.

Castaneda, Carlos, *The Power of Silence*, New York, NY: Simon and Schuster, 1987.

Cho, Paul Yonggi, *The Fourth Dimension*, South Plainfield, NJ: Bridge Publishing, 1979. To go beyond our three-dimensional world we need to develop and refine the way we interact with that world. Dr. Cho gives insights into doing this.

de Becker, Gavin, *The Gift of Fear*, New York, NY: Little Brown & Co, 1997. de Becker shows how intuition is our "gift" and why it's so important to pay attention to it when we experience fear.

Fields, Rick, *The Code of the Warrior*, New York, NY: HarperCollins Publishers, 1991. I've found this book helpful because it gives a history of sorts on the evolution of the warrior.

Gallwey, W. Timothy, *The Inner Game of Tennis*, New York, NY: Random House, 1974. I've found the inner disciplines and strategies of tennis related by Mr. Gallwey to be very applicable to climbing.

Hawkins, David, *Power vs. Force*, Carlsbad, CA: Hay House, 1995. This book gives tangible evidence of the link between our thoughts and our physical power.

Hyams, Joe, *Zen in the Martial Arts*, New York, NY: Bantam Books, 1979. The martial arts are a metaphor for living life on purpose and with more awareness. Combine that with Zen and we achieve a better understanding for flowing with the challenges of life and climbing.

Jampolsky, Gerald G., *Love is Letting Go of Fear*, New York, NY: Bantam Books, 1970. Build on love, don't tear down fear. This book helps us understand how fear-based motivation can diminish as we develop our focus on what we love.

Kabat-Zinn, Jon, *Wherever You Go There You Are*, New York, NY: Hyperion, 1994. The Journey process keeps our attention in the moment. This book helps us understand the importance of paying attention to what is happening NOW.

Little, John, *The Warrior Within: Bruce Lee*, Chicago, IL: Contemporary Books, 1996. Bruce Lee is one of the all-time masters of martial art, meaning that he went well beyond the physical disciple of his art. The mental insights and Zen connections brought out in this book are very helpful.

Lynch, Jerry & Chungliang Al Huang, *Thinking Body, Dancing Mind*, New York, NY: Bantam Books, 1992 . Expectation, focusing, visualizing, fear, intuition—you name the mental discipline and this book addresses it. With a little of everything, this book gives a broad understanding of mental training.

Mares, Théun, *Return of the Warriors*, Cape Town, South Africa: Lionheart Publishing, 1995. Don Juan's teachings in the Castaneda books can be a bit difficult to assimilate and understand. This book presents the Toltec knowledge that don Juan teaches in a very straightforward and understandable way.

Millman, Dan, *Way of the Peaceful Warrior*, Tiburon, CA: H.J. Kramer, 1984. This is one of the cornerstone books of the warriorship literature. It gives insights into all the warrior processes and is fun to read.

Murphy, Michael, *The Future of the Body*, New York, NY: G.P. Putnam's Sons, 1992. To grow mentally we need to expand our perceptions. This book provides a wealth of information on various techniques and disciplines that help us do so.

Murphy, Shane, *The Achievement Zone*, New York, NY: The Berkeley Publishing Co, 1996. We can learn a lot from sport psychologists and how they help Olympians perform their best. This book does just that.

Musashi, Miyamoto, *The Book of Five Rings*, Boston, MA: Shambhala Publications, 1993. The samurai is the legendary Japanese warrior who faced death daily. To do this effectively he had to let go of his fear of dying and focus on fighting well. This is a landmark book for the samurai mindset.

Osho, *Courage: The Joy of Living Dangerously*, New York, NY: St. Martin's Press, 1999. The comfort zone is great, but we cannot be fully alive by staying there. This book gives remarkable insights into developing courage to enter the risk zone.

Peale, Norman Vincent, *The Power of Positive Thinking*, NY: Balantine Books, 1952. This is an important book for understanding the power that resides within us. It will help improve awareness of how to tap that power.

Peck, M. Scott, *The Road Less Traveled*, New York, NY: Simon and Schuster, 1978. All paths begin at a fork in the road. We must decide not to walk the path of the ordinary person in order to begin walking the warrior path. This is a great book for beginning that process.

Sanchez, Victor, *The Teachings of don Carlos*, Santa Fe, NM: Bear and Company Publishing, 1995. This book gives practical applications to the Toltec teachings in the Castaneda books. I've found it very practical and useful when applied to climbing.

Spencer, Robert L., *The Craft of the Warrior*, Berkeley, CA: Frog Ltd, 1993. There are countless writers on warriorship. Mr. Spencer compiles many of them in this book and ties the warrior principles together in a very helpful way. A must read.

Tolle, Eckhart, *The Power of Now*, Novato, CA: New World Library, 1999. The Journey process involves keeping our attention on the task at hand. This book shows the power of being focused in the NOW and gives insights into how to do it.

Trungpa, Chögyam, *Shambhala: The Sacred Path of the Warrior*, Boston, MA: Shambhala Publications, 1984. The Shambhala knowledge from Tibet can help us see the underlying goodness of how the world works. This knowledge helps us accept situations as they are, rather than resist them, so we can deal with them powerfully.

Watts, Alan, *The Way of Zen*, New York: Pantheon, 1957. Zen helps us see situations from new perspectives, and helps us live in the present moment. Dr. Watts is an important author for introducing Zen to the West.

Wolinsky, Stephen, *The Tao of Chaos*, Bearsville, NY: Bramble Books, 1994. Focus on fear and we attract more fear. Quantum Psychology takes us to the building blocks of our mental framework and helps us understand how our mindset creates this unwanted attraction.

Audiotape Programs

Chopra, Deepak, *The Higher Self*, Niles, IL: Nightingale Conant, 1992. To improve awareness we need to diminish the Ego, or better yet, develop the awareness of our higher self. This program can help.

Dossey, Larry, *The Power of Prayer*, Niles, IL: Nightingale Conant, 1994.
Our thoughts have power. This program is a provocative study of scientific experiments on the power of our thoughts.

Dyer, Wayne, *Freedom Through Higher Awareness*, Niles, IL: Nightingale Conant, 1994. Transcend the Ego and we improve our awareness and our power. With more power we have more freedom to choose our actions. This program is a must.

Levey, Joel & Michelle, *The Focused Mind State*, Niles, IL: Nightingale Conant, 1993. Based on the Trojan Warrior Project for the U.S. Army, this program addresses the need to have a focused mind and how to develop it.

Lewis, Dennis, *Breathing as a Metaphor for Living*, Boulder, CO: Sounds True, 1998. How you breathe gives insights into how you live life or how you climb. This program is a powerful guide to better breathing and awareness.

Pulos, Lee, *The Power of Visualization*, Niles, IL: Nightingale Conant, 1993. Visualization is an important tool for developing mental skills. This program goes into the details of this process.

Viscott, David, *Taking Risks*, Niles, IL: Nightingale Conant, 1991. Understanding fear and the need to take risks develops our mental skills. This program addresses these issues and more.

Walther, George, *Power Talk*, Boulder, CO: Career Track, 1991. How we speak to others and ourselves determines the actions we take. This program helps develop a more deliberate way of communicating.

Weil, Andrew, *Breathing*, Boulder, CO: Sounds True, 1999. This program covers important background information on breathing and gives specific exercises that can help improve the quality of our breath.

Wolinsky, Stephen, *Waking from the Trance*, Boulder, CO: Sounds True, 2002. One of the most important tasks for a warrior is becoming more aware. This program addresses how we are socialized into a trance and helps us to wake from that trance.

About the Author

Arno Ilgner was introduced to climbing in 1973 and has been actively involved since then, climbing in areas across the US and Canada, and in France and Korea. Some of his significant first ascents include the 1100-foot east face of Cloud Peak in the Big Horn Mountains of Wyoming, the team free ascent of *Glass Menagerie* on the north face of Looking Glass Rock in North Carolina, and numerous headwall routes on Whitesides Mountain, also in North Carolina.

Arno has developed his Rock Warrior's Way mental training method over the course of ten years, working with hundreds of students. He also teaches courses on movement that help climbers improve their balance and create more energy-efficient performances. He lives with his family in Tennessee and conducts courses mainly in the Southeast, but also travels to other areas of the country to teach clinics and make presentations. Climbers have attended his courses from as far away as Canada, California, Florida, and New York. Recently he has been working with young competition climbers.

Visit his web site **www.warriorsway.com** to sign up for the Rock Warrior's Way mailing list and to receive the free quarterly eNewsletter.